Media Handbook

Contents

The Open University
Walton Hall
Milton Keynes MK7 6AA

First published 1996. Reprinted 1999, 2000

Copyright © 1996 The Open University

Edited and designed by The Open University

Printed in the United Kingdom by Page Bros, Norwich

ISBN 0 7492 7705 X

1.3

Introduction

The twelve programmes which comprise *The Shape of the World* television series offer a rather different experience of geography from that of the written teaching materials, in so far as they attempt to bring alive in a direct way many of the issues and themes laid out in the course as a whole. The two – the written course materials and the programmes – are complementary; they are intended as part of an integrated teaching package which allows you the possibility to consider the same topic or issue through images as well as texts. The programmes are spread evenly through the course, relating to a particular chapter or chapters within a specific volume.

More significantly, however, the programmes also relate to one another as a series. As you watch them, a broader picture of the contemporary world is built up through a succession of topics and images which exemplify some of the more important developments which shape peoples' lives in a global context. Central to the series is the ability to think about such developments in a geographical manner; that is, to exercise our geographical imaginations on events and issues which are shaping both the social and the natural environment around us.

The first programme, 'Imagining new worlds', takes its cue directly from this theme, involving you in a journey through eastern Mexico that asks you to think carefully about how the place has been interpreted and understood by different people over time and in the present day. From there the series takes you all over the world, and asks you to think about, for instance, the anger expressed by many indigenous Hawaiians over the gross commercialization of their culture through global tourism, or the plight of Alaskan peoples today attempting to live their lives in what many see simply as wild, 'empty' spaces, or the nature of water conflicts in the US and beyond, or the political anxiety of falling population numbers in Italy, or how the 'world' enters world music in Mali in Central Africa or even how the western imagination makes sense of China's growing importance on the economic world stage. In each of the programmes, you will find it useful to reflect upon and to gather your impressions about how different peoples understand the world and their place within it.

Indeed, each of the programmes and the accompanying notes in this Media Handbook have been designed to be *used actively*; that is, as a resource to be drawn upon which enhances your understanding of the course as a whole and in relation to specific assignments. The notes which accompany each programme have been set out in a similar way, under the headings of aims and links, programme content, and related teaching activities. The aims and links give you both a sense of the questions addressed in the programme and how they relate to particular chapters and volumes in the course. You should ensure that you read them carefully before viewing a programme. The programme content sets out the sequence and storyline of the material, whilst the activities are designed to alert you to any preparatory reading and the kinds of issues and ideas to look out for as the programme progresses. The activities also include prompts to consider after viewing the programme as to the broader significance of many of the issues raised, both within the programme series and the course as a whole. Some of the prompts are simply intended to be thought-provoking in a general sense, while others key you more closely into the main ideas and themes of the course.

The programme notes may also be of value to you in other ways too – for example, if you miss a programme and are unable to record it or borrow a recording from your Regional Centre. In such circumstances, the notes provide a useful and informative summary of the programme's aims and content which should help you to include ideas or illustrations from them in your assignments and in your examination answers.

However you choose to use this Media Handbook, we hope that the series opens up in a very direct and immediate sense a world that is taking shape around us and of which we are all a part.

John Allen

D215 Course Team Chair

TV1   'Imagining new worlds'

Academic consultant: Doreen Massey

Producer: Eleanor Morris

1   Aims/links

This programme explores one of the central concepts of the course: the geographical imagination. What it aims to do, above all, is bring this notion alive for you by exploring it in detail in a real-world context. We have done this by presenting the story of a journey through eastern Mexico. I went there to find out about this place, but what I discovered was that there are many ways of imagining it – that is, of interpreting its character as a place, of placing it within a wider 'global' world, and of characterizing its natural environment. The programme thus links very directly into Volume 1 Chapter 1, 'Imagining the world', and you should make sure you have read this chapter thoroughly before you watch the programme. In particular you should check that you know your way around two of the key concepts of that chapter: *geographical imagination* and *contested views of space, place and nature.*

The programme includes a section about a native American indigenous society, that of the modern Maya, and some aspects of their struggle for survival as a culture in the face of a world-view dominated by investors in the global production of products and exploitation of resources. This clearly touches on some of the same issues as does the case study of coastal Honduras with which the chapter opens, and you may like to run over that discussion before you view the programme.

There are two other key concepts of Chapter 1 which are also explored in the programme: you will find further discussion of what we mean by the term *hybrid culture,* and some further implicit questioning of the terms *the local and the global.* Finally, this is a region which, after the arrival of Columbus in the Americas, was invaded by the Spanish. What they found – and attempted to destroy – was a flourishing culture, but one very different from their own. Today, the new explorers, from whose point of view the programme begins, are the thousands of tourists, especially from abroad, who arrive every year. For both these groups, and for me myself as I arrive in Cancún, what is at issue is a *voyage of discovery* and, as so often, what are discovered are both 'new worlds' and new ways of imagining the world.

2   The programme

This programme picks up three themes from Volume 1 Chapter 1. They are:

o   the geographical imagination (this is the overall theme of the programme)

o   hybrid cultures

o   the local and the global.

2.1 The geographical imagination

The programme traces a journey of discovery in south-eastern Mexico: see Figure 1. It explores different ways in which people have imagined this place and represented it, how they have thought about and related to its natural environment, and how they have set this region within a wider geographical context.

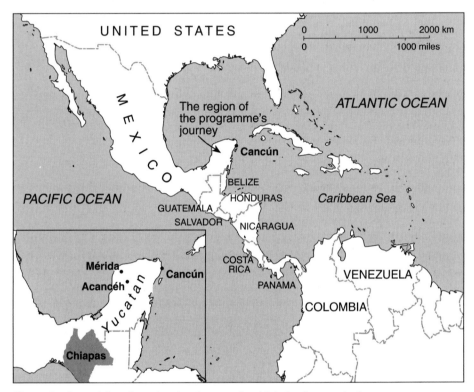

Figure 1 Central America, showing the area in which the journey in the programme was made

Four views are explored – those of tourists, classical Mayans, modern Mayans and corporate capital.

1 The tourist view

We begin in Cancún, and with the tourists' view of this region as being a place of leisure, a place to relax. Crucially, it is a place away from 'the real world' of work and humdrum daily life. The 'nature' which the tourists seek here is sun, sea, sand and palm trees, blended into some generalized notion of 'the Caribbean'.

Yet even here, among the modern hotels, we get indications that there have been, and maybe still are, other understandings of this place ... an ancient Mayan pyramid, like the hotels, looks out to sea, and in the gardens of the hotels the gardeners, for whom this definitely *is* the real world of daily work and life, speak Yucatec Mayan and clip into the hedges symbolic shapes derived from another culture.

2   The classical Mayan view

The most impressive thing to emerge here is the complexity of the Mayan geographical imagination. It has a number of aspects.

First, the Maya were able to make advanced astronomical measurements. They could predict planetary movements, the positions of sun and moon and so forth, with great accuracy.

However, this knowledge was placed at the service of a cosmological understanding that was very different from our own (we saw a similar phenomenon in Chapter 1 of Volume 1 in discussion of the Babylonians). This understanding was of a layered cosmos, where the Earth on which we live was a thin layer set amongst others. The layers were held together by figures at the four cardinal points, each signifying a particular relation to nature (as illustrated on the Mérida mural). This, then, is a map, like the Babylonian one and like all other maps, which establishes the place of this people in the wider sphere. And, in this view, the Mayan country is at the centre of the world.

This view is thus quite unlike the tourist view, on a number of counts:

(a) It is built on different principles.

It is a map with much in common with European *mappae mundi*; it is a religious framing of the world. It is also a map with both time and space represented: the *mappae mundi* told the stories of Christianity (see section 1.2.1 of Volume 1); the Mayan maps (such as those woven into the *huipiles* in Chiapas) tell the story of the passage of the sun between dusk and dawn, or the story of the landscape and the weather, on which depends life itself.

(b) This place is at the centre of the world.

In this view, the classical Mayan geographical imagination is quite unlike that of the tourists, in whose view of the world this region is on the periphery and apart from the real world.

(c) It is based on a different interpretation of nature.

In the cosmic map, the story is also told of the birth of human beings from corn (maize). For the Maya, human beings and nature are utterly interrelated. People have animal counterparts; corn is both the stuff of life and represented in a god; the landscape itself is alive. (When we were there filming, it was easy to appreciate this view, as the clouds mingled with the mountains in an unending movement, as people spoke of earthquakes and volcanoes, as we heard at night the constant unknown noise of the forest.) In such a context the Earth cannot belong to anybody; rather we belong to the Earth. It is Mother Earth – *la Madre Tierra*.

But the classical Maya also had other ways of placing themselves in the wider world:

o   their political connections, and the region which can properly be called Maya, stretched from this part of Mexico south through Belize, Guatemala and Honduras. (Note, immediately, that it ignored the boundaries of today's nation-states – see Chapter 1, section 1.1.3, Box 1.1.)

o   there was also an extensive set of trading connections, which must have stretched, through direct and indirect connections, from Arizona in the United States to Colombia in South America. To maintain such connections, some knowledge of terrestrial geography as we think of it must have existed. There was thus co-existence of cosmological and trading representations of the world, just as in the Middle Ages the *mappae mundi* co-existed with portolan charts (Chapter 1, section 1.2.1).

The Maya, indeed, drew a map for the conquistador Hernán Cortés (though it was a map for people on foot not on horses, which were unknown to the Maya).

3   The modern Mayan view

The arrival of the Spanish, on a classic 'voyage of discovery', did much to destroy what remained of Mayan culture. But it by no means destroyed it entirely. In the Mayan life of this region today there remain many elements of this culture. The programme gives evidence of a number of these elements that are still important:

o   indigenous clothes

o   traditional weaving designs

o   the belief in a communal relation to land

o   the deep appreciation of the importance of the elements

o   maize and its centrality

o   the general attitude towards the natural world.

This is a 'hybrid' view, to which we shall return below.

4   Corporate capital's view

This term stands for the 'modern' globalizing economy, into which the Mayan lands are being increasingly incorporated. Bishop Samuel Ruiz talks of this and links it to the neo-liberal free trade policies of the Mexican and other governments. In this view, Mayan lands are seen in terms of their investment potential, its nature in terms of exploitable resources (Chiapas is already a major provider of hydro-electric power to other regions). This is a view of the world which thinks in terms of profit and divides it up according to an international division of labour. Apart from being exploited for its 'natural resources', the current view is that, on this understanding of the world – this geographical imagination – the Mayan lands, and especially Chiapas, will once again be seen as 'peripheral'.

There are, then, different ways of imagining and representing this region of the world and its nature.

Note also five other points:

(a) These different geographical imaginations are related to the position of the people who hold them.

(b) There can be differences even in one society. The tourists and corporate capital, both parts of 'the modern world', have differing views; in Mayan society it was the elites who held the knowledge of the world.

(c) Such elite views of the world can be influential in a society, become widely accepted, and even hold it together. Peter Matthews explains that this seems to have been the case with the ancient Maya. You may want to consider in a similar light today's 'free-trade' views of the world as a global market and place of production.

(d) The fact that these different views of the world exist matters: it has effects; frequently it leads to contestation. Bishop Landa in the sixteenth century quite explicitly tried to eradicate many features of Mayan civilization which he saw as being against (his) God. Most significantly in the programme we see the confrontation between Mayan peoples today and other views of the world. A clear example is the recent change made to the Mexican constitution. This formally opens up *ejido* (communal) land to private ownership. It is a measure designed to increase the possibilities of profitable investment, but it cuts right across the Mayan view of land as something that cannot be owned by individuals.

(e) Moreover, when cultures meet, they often interpret each other in their own terms. Thus, as Blanca de Mariscal points out, the manuscripts that Landa left us interpret Mayan religion through Spanish eyes.

Painting of Bishop Landa, a sixteenth-century priest, suffering auto-da-fé. Because he destroyed original evidence, his writings became the only source of knowledge about Mayan civilization, but they are a particular interpretation

2.2 Hybrid cultures

All cultures are to some extent hybrid – the modern architecture of Cancún picks up on ancient Mayan influences; global capital may well adapt in some of its ways to local conditions. As the tourist says on the bus: 'people aren't separated'. But the present-day culture of this region of Mexico exhibits hybridity in particularly clear forms. There are numerous examples in the programme:

o   Blanca de Mariscal's discussion of 'syncretism' – the mutual influencing of Spanish and Mayan cultures, each incorporating aspects of the other.

o   The corn ceremony where Mayan language and beliefs are enacted by men in jeans, trainers and baseball caps.

o   The village of Acancéh where a modern-day Mayan market sits in the same square as a centuries-old Catholic Church and an even older pyramid. Even the physical form of this little town manifests its hybridity.

o   The women in the village near Mayapán, making tortillas in a manner just like their forebears. But in the front are three video-game machines, and the women talk of their children who go to work in Mérida and then come back home – children who bridge two worlds.

An illustration of the hybridity of cultures – the man is wearing modern clothes, but is speaking the Mayan language and conducting an old Mayan ceremony just prior to harvesting the corn

2.3   The local and the global

The programme also implicitly raises issues about the constitution of, and the relation between, the global and the local – and, as does Chapter 1, it hints at some of the complexities involved in these apparently simple terms. As one way into this issue, try to relate the struggle in Chiapas to the Honduran case in Chapter 1. Thus:

o   At the most immediate level, this is a struggle of a local people against global capital and political and economic policies of globalization.

o   Yet the local people are in fact more complicated in their origins and characteristics than simply 'local'. For one thing, as the woman on the bus has learned, the Maya originally hail from Asia; they are not, in some ultimate sense, of local origin. Moreover, as we also see, their culture is now a complex mix of influences from many parts of the world. Even the ancient Maya had contacts with what are now the USA and South America. And today's Maya are even more complex, combining influences from Spanish, modern-day Mexican and 'international-modern' cultures.

o   What is more, they realize the value of 'going beyond the local' in their struggle. The Bishop talked to me also of a new realization of a common Mayan history and heritage which links together different groups. He also spoke, beyond that, of a wider movement, and coming together, of indigenous people from around the world and the internationalization of their local struggles.

Activities

Before the programme

This programme links directly to Volume 1 Chapter 1, so do make sure you have read the first chapter of the course!

After the programme

1   Make sure you can encapsulate briefly the distinct geographical imaginations of the different groups/societies. You might find the following format useful to organize your thoughts:

	Place	Space*	Nature
Tourists			
Maya			
Corporate capital			

Note: *By 'space' here we are mainly referring to the location of this place within a wider global setting.

2   Make sure you can explain how, in very general terms, these different geographical imaginations are related to the position of the people who hold them.

3   Why is 'geographical imagination' an important concept? What kind of effects can result from the fact that geographical imaginations may vary? Give an example from the programme, and also one other – either from Chapter 1 or from outside the course.

4   Run through the points in section 2.3 above, relating the Zapatista struggle in Chiapas to the Honduran case in Chapter 1.

TV2   'Reflections on a global screen'

Academic consultant: Chris Hamnett

Producer: Eleanor Morris

1   Aims/links

Globalization can take a variety of different forms. This programme examines one of its most powerful and potent forms – the globalization of news and entertainment through television. The images and values it offers are widely available for the cost of a receiver and a licence or a reception fee.

Until relatively recently, television production and broadcasting have been concentrated in the advanced western countries and, American imports not withstanding, most western countries had their major national television channels, such as the BBC in Britain. But globalization is leading to three main trends: first, the development of global media corporations active in a variety of sectors and a variety of global regions; secondly, the globalization of markets; and, thirdly, the development of new technologies such as satellites, which can broadcast across the world.

The globalization of mass media is a specific example of the processes discussed by Andrew Leyshon in Chapter 1 of *A Shrinking World?* These were time–space convergence, time–space distanciation and time–space compression. Technology is bringing different parts of the world closer together in time terms, ownership and control are concentrated in other countries, and the whole process is speeding up and widening out as producers and distributors seek greater profits and a wider market.

2   The programme

The thesis of the programme is that we are witnessing the globalization of film and TV, as a result of three interrelated processes. The *first* is the rise of large-scale, integrated worldwide media empires such as Time Warner, CNN, Murdoch's News Corp, Sony and Bertelsmann. These corporations are expanding their ownership of production and distribution across a wide range of media via a series of mergers and take-overs. They are engaged in a process of vertical and horizontal integration. Thus Sony bought up Columbia Pictures and Tri-Star as well as CBS records, and Time Corporation took over Warner Bros; the merging of Time Warner and CNN was announced in September 1995. Matsushita (the Japanese electronics company) now owns MCA pictures, and News Corp have bought Star TV in Hong Kong.

Corporate media empires dominate the global film and television industry

The *second* element in this process of globalization is the development of global markets: these corporations need to be in all the world's key markets to ensure maximum profitability. This is leading to the expansion of the major companies into a wide variety of different countries. Time Warner, for example, has just opened an office in Shanghai, and the rapidly developing South East Asian market is seen to be particularly attractive as economic development leads to a growing middle class of prosperous consumers.

The *third* element is the emergence of new distribution technologies which permit much larger potential markets to be reached. Two are of particular importance: fibre-optic cables and satellite TV. The former are often more important in western countries – witness the cabling of much of London – and the latter is important in developing regions such as Asia.

The programme starts by looking at the traditional role of Hollywood as the main centre of the world's film and television industry (Bombay and Hong Kong are important also-rans). Hollywood was traditionally organized around the studios, but all of them have now been taken over: Warner Bros by Time; Columbia and Tri-Star by Sony; Fox by News Corp; Disney by Buena Vista; MCA by Matsushita; MGM is owned by Credit Lyonnais; and, most recently, Paramount has been bought by Viacom.

The programme asks why these take-overs have occurred. The answer is that the hardware and distribution companies need product, and Hollywood is still the major centre of film and television production. It is no good owning a satellite system if you have nothing to broadcast. The studios also have vast libraries of old films which can provide hours of entertainment to fill the schedules cheaply.

The development and structure of the Hollywood film industry is examined in an interview with Alan Scott, and the global strategy of one of the majors is explored through an interview with Barbara Bragliotti, the head of TV PR for Warner. She outlines Warner's global strategy and argues that it is now important to achieve global sales and distribution as production costs have risen to such an extent that it is virtually impossible to recover costs by sales within the US. Though a strong home base is important, global sales are necessary for profits. As an example, we look at filming of the television series, *The New Adventures of Superman*, which is sold to more than thirty countries, including Japan.

Time Warner is one of the major companies in the global media industry, but the BBC is determined to capitalize on the global brand name and the existence of BBC World Service Radio through the development of a new joint venture – World Wide Television (WWTV) – with the Pearson company (who own the Financial Times and Longman Publishers among others). From its base in London, WWTV is currently broadcasting in Japanese and in Mandarin Chinese and has also established its own Arabic service. The BBC news is dubbed into various languages by World Service News and is then transmitted via satellite.

On the set of The New Adventures of Superman – *using a global icon to reap worldwide sales*

Bob Phillis, the Deputy Director General of the BBC, and Hugh Williams, the Director of Programmes for BBC WWTV, outline the strategy for getting the BBC into the global market and expanding its coverage worldwide.

The second part of the programme was shot in Hong Kong at the first MIP Asia conference (an Asian equivalent of the Cannes Film Festival) where film and TV producers, buyers and distributors come together to buy and sell and discuss strategies for the development of the global media market. The theme of the conference was *Many Cultures, One Market – Towards a Global Industry.*

Among the topics covered are the following:

1   An interview with Time Warner executives to examine their global goals and objectives.

2   The expansion of Music TV (MTV) into Europe and Asia, including interviews with some of the key executives. MTV is a major force for cultural globalization, although they are promoting Asian bands and stars in South East Asia as well as western ones.

3   We look at the struggle to gain control of the South East Asian satellite TV market based in Hong Kong. When News Corp bought Star TV (which broadcasts into India and China) it fought off the British Pearson Group which has now joined with BBC to form World Wide TV. An alternative station (TVB) is also in operation.

4   A final strand in the story we look at is the fact that the flow of news and programmes is not all one-way (from the west to the east). There are two stations in Hong Kong which produce/distribute China news which is

sent by cassette (but soon satellite) to Europe and the West coast of the USA for distribution to the Chinese diaspora. The globalization of television is not a uni-directional process.

One point made in the programme is that it is impossible simply to take western programmes and transmit them. While some programme types (news or nature programmes) can easily be dubbed into other languages, there is a need for local programming, and global media corporations are beginning to make programmes locally. Thus MTV Asia features many home-grown bands and stars as well as ubiquitous western stars. We explore this and some of the current political issues raised by beaming in western programming to Asian countries with different political and cultural systems. This raises the question of the extent to which global television can (a) change politics and cultures, and (b) be controlled and resisted.

Activities

Before the programme

Ideally, you should have read Andrew Leyshon's Chapter 1 in Volume 2, 'Annihilating space: the speed-up of communications', before viewing the programme. Think about the extent to which you are exposed to global media in the form of films and television programmes.

During the programme

Critically assess the views and arguments put forward by the various participants. To what extent is globalization of TV simply driven by a desire for greater profitability and global influence?

After the programme

Critically assess the argument that the globalization of mass media involves three key elements:

(a) global production and ownership;

(b) global marketing; and

(c) the existence of global technologies for distribution.

To what extent is globalization of television likely to lead to the development of a common global culture, and would this be desirable?

TV3 'Global firms and the industrializing East'

Academic consultant: John Allen

Producer: Jack Leathem

1 Aims/links

The main aim of the programme is to explore the changing organization of production of multinational corporations and how, through their location decisions, they constantly reshape the divisions of labour laid down between countries. The geographical setting for this exploration is East Asia, and it centres on the changing role of Singapore in the region and the activities of the 4,000 multinationals to which it plays host. Two multinational firms – one, an Italian/French microelectronics multinational, SGS-Thompson, and the other, a finance house dating back to colonial times, the Hong Kong and Shanghai Banking Corporation – carry much of the storyline. In particular, the two firms provide an illustration of how divisions of labour across the globe change in response to changing production technologies, changing skill requirements and the growth of new markets.

The programme is linked directly to Chapter 2 of Volume 2, 'Crossing borders: footloose multinationals?', and its concern with the stretching of social relations across space more generally. Whereas Chapter 2 is concerned with both direct and indirect forms of involvement by multinational firms, however, the programme is more specifically about the types of overseas investment raised in section 2.5. As you watch the programme, you should bear in mind that wider issues discussed in the chapter, especially those of global regions and global interdependence, are of crucial significance to an understanding of the nature of MNCs today.

2 The programme

The significance of Singapore as a site of foreign investment can be traced back to its 'founding' as a free port by the British in 1819 and its historical role as an entrepôt trading centre under British colonial rule for the South East Asia region (see Figure 2). Much of the investment during the colonial era, as pointed out in section 2.2.1 of Volume 2, involved natural resources of one kind or another, and in this context Singapore performed the role of regional centre for capital invested in mining and agriculture in nearby countries such as Malaysia and Indonesia. As such, Singapore's financial and commercial infrastructure developed on the basis of its ability to serve foreign capital investment in the region.

After separation from Malaysia in 1965, the city-state sought to change its role from that of a conduit for capital in the region to that of a site of foreign capital investment in its own right. Today, the economy of Singapore is dominated by foreign-owned multinationals, both manufacturing and service-based, but the bundle of *location factors* that attracted MNCs in the 1960s and 1970s are not the same as those which keep them in Singapore in the 1990s. As the programme shows, the

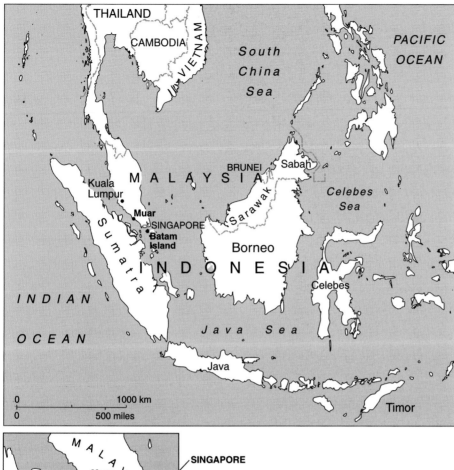

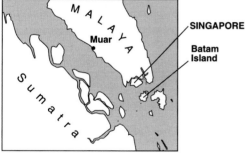

Figure 2 South East Asia, showing the location of Singapore and Batam Island, and Muar in Malaysia

location factors for a number of industries are different and so, too, are the divisions of labour laid down by the MNCs in South East Asia.

2.1 From offshore haven to regional hub

Back in the late 1960s, when the Singapore government set out to attract multinational investment, the main attraction of the city-state to overseas firms was as a relatively cheap, off-shore base from which to export products back to their home markets. With a non-interventionist government, with no regulations governing ownership, the transfer of technology or local content rules, and with an abundant supply of relatively cheap labour, Singapore – along with Hong Kong, Taiwan and

South Korea – experienced a rapid increase in foreign capital investment, especially in the field of electronics and textiles.

Both these industries, because of the nature of technological development within them, are able to split their production processes into a number of discrete parts, of which the relatively standardized, assembly-type operations could be re-located to low-cost locations in the less developed countries, whilst the more skilled work remained in the first world, alongside the multinationals' HQs. It was this fragmentation of manufacturing production which attracted the label of 'the new international division of labour' – new in the sense that it went beyond the division of labour between manufacturing countries and those countries which provided the raw materials and resources. A *spatial division of labour* was now present *within* manufacturing production rather than between firms and industries.

SGS-Thompson, the microelectronics multinational based in Europe, along with other mainly US firms in the electronics industry, was a typical example of this emergent spatial division of labour. With its head offices in France and Italy and its research and development functions concentrated in Europe, the company set up a manufacturing operation in Singapore in 1969 as part of its worldwide search for low-cost assembly locations. In the programme, the current vice-president of SGS-Thompson Asia-Pacific, Milivoj von Somogy, recalls the importance of Singapore as a cheap location for 'back-end' microelectronics work. 'Back-end' refers to the routine, labour-intensive assembly side of semiconductor production – the soldering or fixing of microchips onto printed circuit boards, for example – which can be undertaken by workers with little training or

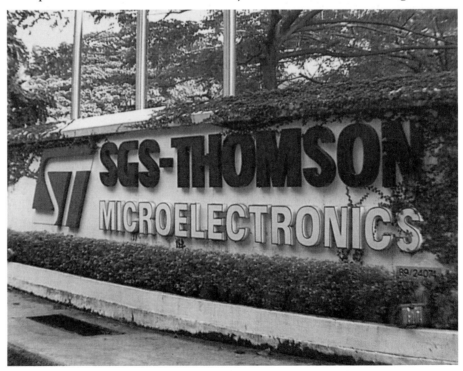

SGS-Thompson's wafer fabrication plant in Singapore – a state-of-the-art European microelectronics factory in South East Asia

industrial experience. These 'global factories', as they are referred to in Chapter 2, were not geared up to produce for the local market but for regional markets elsewhere, in Europe and the US in particular.

The nature of Singapore's attractions to the likes of multinationals such as SGS-Thompson has altered since the late 1960s, however. As von Somogy also remarks, it is the significance of East Asia as a marketplace for semiconductors which now keeps electronics multinationals firmly in Singapore. East Asia, as the world's fastest growing economic region, has become an increasingly competitive marketplace and this requires a production presence within the region to gain market share. Proximity to the market is now a prime consideration and Singapore offers that possibility to western multinationals. Being 'inside' the East Asia global region, however, has also altered the nature of the production presence for multinationals like SGS-Thompson. Singapore is no longer simply a cheap off-shore haven. Its role in the global division of labour has shifted.

If we think about this shift in terms of changes in the division of labour stretched across space, then it is possible to identify from the programme Singapore's altered role and its place within the spatial hierarchy of control and production in firms such as SGS-Thompson. For example:

o   Singapore is now the site of one of SGS-Thompson's wafer fabrication plants, the 'front-end' work that requires skilled labour and state-of-the-art technology.

o   As a result, much of the firm's 'back-end' work has shifted elsewhere within the region, to low-cost locations such as Malaysia and Indonesia.

o   The development of 'core' technologies and the allocation of production and investment is still undertaken at SGS-Thompson sites in Europe, although some local design and research to meet the needs of the East Asian market is carried out in Singapore.

The spatial hierarchy of firms like SGS-Thompson is therefore more complex than before, with a *deeper integration* of their activities within the East Asia market. That said, however, other places within the region have taken on the role of low-wage locations for SGS-Thompson. One such location is Muar in Malaysia.

Global factories revisited?

Places like Muar in Malaysia, some 200 kilometres north of Singapore, fulfil the role that the city-state performed in the late 1960s and 1970s. Much of the workforce in SGS-Thompson's 'back-end' operations in Muar are young, single women with no previous industrial experience. Significantly, they are paid at a fraction of the rate obtainable in more developed locations in East Asia to perform low-skilled, routine operations. Here, however, the similarity starts to fade. For what characterizes 'back-end' work today in places like Muar is that, in common with 'front-end' work, much of the production is based upon capital-intensive, state-of-the-art-technology. SGS-Thompson's plant in Malaysia is not a labour-intensive operation, but rather a combination of expensive machinery *and* cheap labour. Moreover, the export market served is that of East Asia, rather than Europe or the US.

This is not to suggest, however, that 'global factories' are a thing of the past, merely that in semiconductor production the whole process has become more capital-intensive and orientated to regional markets. In other sectors, in consumer electronics, for example, 'global factories' are still in evidence, as the case of Batam Industrial Park in Indonesia illustrates.

Batam Industrial Park – a short ferry ride from Singapore – offers MNCs Indonesia's vast land and labour resources coupled with Singapore's industrial management

Some 20 kilometres south of Singapore, the Batam Industrial Park is located on Pulau Batam, an island of the Riau Province. The Park opened in 1991 and now plays host to just under 50 companies from the Netherlands, France, Germany, Switzerland, Italy, the UK, the US, Singapore Malaysia, South Korea and Japan. There are presently around 22,000 workers employed there, a figure which is expected to rise to 50,000 on completion of the Park in 1996. The majority of the workforce are young, single women, mostly drawn from other Indonesian islands on a renewable, fixed-term contract basis. Unlike Muar, however, much of the work is labour-intensive and for re-export on the world market, particularly in those operations owned by European and US multinationals.

What is also of interest about such a development is its relationship to Singapore. The Singapore government, in the shape of one of its companies, Singapore Technologies Industrial Corporation (STIC), in partnership with others, has built and currently runs the Park. This is part of a conscious attempt by the Singapore city-state to 'upgrade' its own economy, whilst channelling low-cost, labour-intensive work to neighbouring countries. This attempt to 'upgrade' is also apparent in the city-state's financial operations.

2.3   As a financial centre

From its past role as a regional financial and offshore banking centre, Singapore has carved out for itself a particular role in the global financial division of labour, as a centre of currency and futures business in the East Asia region. Aided by developments in communications technology and the growth of the East Asia market, Singapore has great hopes of becoming a global financial centre – and in one sense it already is – although for the exchange of foreign currency rather than as a major capital market. If anything, Singapore's entrepôt status is highlighted by such developments and in the programme you should listen carefully to what those from the Hong Kong and Shanghai Bank have to say about Singapore's changing financial role.

2.4   Looking to East Asia

The final part of the programme draws attention briefly to the recognition, both by 'third world' multinationals from within East Asia itself and by western firms located in Singapore, that the East Asia market will increasingly be the focus of their activities. China, in particular, is referred to as both a potentially massive market and as a cheap labour location for multinational firms.

Connections (*guanxi*) between the Chinese-speaking group in Singapore, in particular the Hokkien Chinese, and mainland China are regarded as important networks for Singapore firms and also for western multinationals to tap into through their Singapore partners. Whatever the success of such a strategy, the programme ends with a sense of what shape economic globalization in the 'East' may take (an issue which is taken up more forcefully in TV12).

Activities

Before the programme

Ideally, you should have read Chapter 2, 'Crossing borders: footloose multinationals?', before you view the programme. If you are pushed for time, then section 2.5 is essential reading. Insights from Chapter 1 on finance and telecommunications will also be relevant to the programme.

During the programme

There are two broad aspects that you should think about as you watch the programme:

(a) the way in which different places offer certain advantages and disadvantages to multinational firms at any particular time, depending upon changing technologies, wage levels and markets especially;

(b) a related point to bear in mind is how the spatial division of labour between countries – in both manufacturing and finance – has altered over time – and why.

After the programme

Spend a few minutes trying to get down on paper the changing role of Singapore in East Asia and more widely since the mid-1960s. Then think about the following in relation to the above two points:

o   Have you understood what is meant by a *spatial division of labour* and such notions as a 'global factory' (and 'front-end' and 'back-end' operations)?

o   Have you grasped the significance of *location factors* to multinational firms?

o   And, perhaps a more difficult one to think through, what forms of *interdependence* laid down by global firms did you note?

o   Finally, what do you understand by the term *global region* in relation to East Asia?

TV4   'Global tourism'

Academic consultant: Chris Hamnett

Producer: Eleanor Morris

1   Aims/links

As Erlet Cater points out in Chapter 5 of Volume 2, *A Shrinking World?*, tourism is a key aspect of economic and cultural globalization. Hundreds of millions of people travel the globe every year for recreational holidays and 'to see the world'. Tourism is now one of the world's major industries, generating massive revenues and providing a major source of employment in some parts of the world. But, as Cater points out, tourism is not an unmitigated benefit. Although it brings development of a certain kind, it has major environmental, social and cultural impacts on many destination areas.

This programme examines the growth of global tourism, and the social and cultural problems it generates. Its focus is on the role of tourism in 'shrinking' the world, the constant search for the exotic and the 'unspoilt' and the impact of tourism on indigenous cultures. The aim of the programme is to make you aware of the expanding frontier of global tourism and of some of the problems that it generates.

2   The programme

The programme falls into three major sections, looking at three different locations – Hawaii (especially Honolulu), Malaysia and, finally, the Hawaiian Island of Kauai.

2.1   The impact of mass tourism in Hawaii

The first part of the programme examines the development of mass tourism in Hawaii, since the construction of the first hotels in the early 1900s. It shows how tourism has expanded as a result of the reduction in travel time from the West Coast of continental USA from five days (by ship) to five hours (by modern jet). As access has improved and the relative price of travel has fallen, Hawaii has become one of the major American holiday destinations. Given its position in the centre of the northern Pacific, it is also within relatively easy reach of Japan (7 hours): see Figure 3. As a result, Hawaii is now host to millions of tourists a year, and Waikiki Beach, Honolulu – the major destination area – has experienced massive high-rise hotel development, frequently built on, or adjacent to, new shopping plazas selling clothes, beachwear and a host of other goods.

The programme also examines the way in which the image of Hawaii as an exotic (but safe) tropical paradise for tourists was created and fostered in the inter-war years through the radio programme *Hawaii Calls*: this was broadcast every Sunday for over thirty years from the patio of the Moana Hotel. This programme – with the unmistakable sound of its Hawaiian steel guitars – played a major part in creating an image of Hawaii amongst millions of American listeners who had never visited the Islands. This,

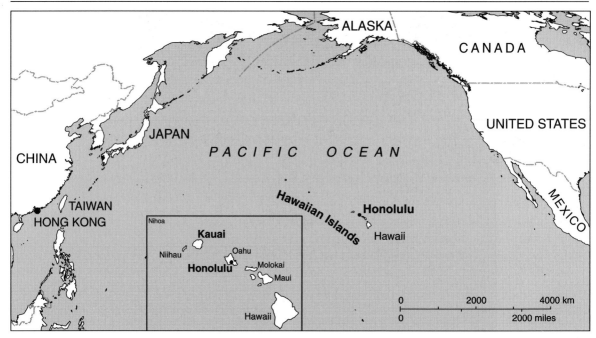

Figure 3 *The Hawaiian Islands, located between North America and East Asia*

together with Elvis Presley's film *Blue Hawaii*, helped to create an image of Hawaii as the home of surfing and hula dancing.

This is still the image which many tourists come to the islands expecting to find. But it is an image which some Hawaiians resent and, as a local Hawaiian explains, they believe that many tourists are getting only an artificial, watered down experience of Hawaiian culture, portrayed through the 'Hawaiian cultural extravaganzas' at the main hotels, ready packaged for tourist consumption.

But away from Waikiki Beach, the reality of Honolulu is one of traffic congestion and high-rise apartments. After one hundred years of American colonialism, there is not much of traditional Hawaiian culture left untouched. Most native Hawaiians are thoroughly Americanized, and many work in tourism or ancillary occupations.

For this reason, and also because of the large numbers of visitors and the high level of tourist development in places like Hawaii, many tourists are seeking more out-of-the-way spots (currently only lightly touched by tourism) for vacations. The aim is to visit places ahead of the development of mass tourism and before they are 'spoilt'.

2.2   The opening up of Malaysia

In the second part of the programme we shift our attention to look at Malaysia – an area of the world which has only relatively recently begun to experience major development of the tourist industry. Some parts of Malaysia, such as Penang Island, seem to be well on the way to 'Hawaiianization', as high-rise beach hotels sprout at a rapid rate. But other parts of Malaysia remain relatively untouched, although even here tourism is taking firm root.

The popular tourist image of Hawaii – a cultural experience removed from what some Hawaiians regard as 'their' culture

The programme travels to Langkawi, an island in the far north-west of Malaysia, on the border with Thailand (see Figure 4). The island is already experiencing considerable development in some parts, but the aim is to control development and ensure that it remains low-rise on the north coast (facing Thailand). An Indonesian company has acquired an area of previously untouched tropical forest (some 2,000 acres) where they have constructed a luxury golf course and hotel, 'The Detai', discreetly built within the rain forest. The aim of the development is to attract wealthy tourists who appreciate the hotel for its location, and the fact that they can watch and hear the birds, monkeys and other wild animals in the trees which surround the hotel. Many of the rooms are in the form of chalets set in the forest and access is either on foot or by electric buggy. No cars are permitted, and the hotel offers guided forest walks.

'The Detai' represents the up-market end of ecotourism and Jamie Case, the manager, thinks this is where the future of tourism lies – in relatively low-impact niche resorts, rather than in the development of mass tourism. But Langkawi now has an international airport capable of taking large jets on direct flights from Europe, Japan and elsewhere. At the time of filming, a marketing manager from the British travel company, Kuoni, was visiting the complex with a view to including it in their future brochures. The pressure towards development is intense and, as the programme shows, some locally run hotels and chalets on prime beachfront sites may be compulsorily purchased by the government to make way for more profitable and up-market hotels and golf courses. The combined pressure of big business and government is difficult to resist.

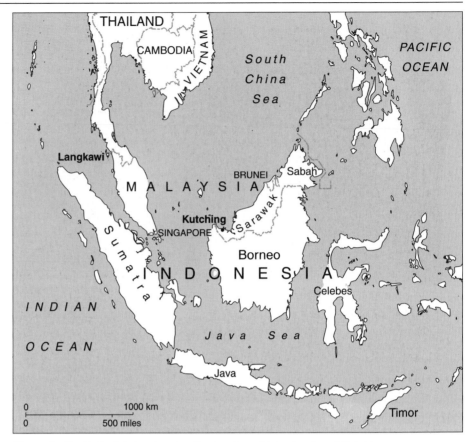

Figure 4 South East Asia, showing the location of Langkawi and Kutching

The programme goes on to look at one of the leading edges of what is sometimes termed 'cultural' or adventure tourism. Sarawak, a state of Malaysia on the island of Borneo, is famous for its legacy of head-hunting tribal peoples, its tropical forest and its animals. It is not conventionally associated with tourism. But where the back-packers lead, tourism often follows, and since the mid 1980s a few local companies have been pioneering trips up-river to visit and stay with the Iban and Dyak tribespeoples in their traditional riverside longhouses.

The trips are still relatively difficult and involve only a few people in 'low-intensity' visits two or three times a week. It is necessary for visitors to stay in the longhouse, or an adjacent hut, in fairly primitive conditions (although running water has recently been brought in from the river by pipe to supply a toilet and washing hut for visitors). The journey takes about six hours from the capital Kutching – five hours by van and then an hour by boat.

The traditional riverside longhouses of the Iban and Dyak tribes – part of a 'cultural tourism' package which may soon experience the impact of mass tourism

The local reaction to tourists seemed very positive in early 1994 when we visited the area. They were able to use the money to buy engine fuel and medicines and to enable their children to go to secondary school (weekly boarding about forty miles away). A journey that used to take two days by canoe now takes about an hour with high-speed outboard engines: this is time–space convergence with a vengeance. But the longhouse we visited had only had visitors for about a year and reactions may differ when numbers begin to increase – as they inevitably will. When we visited, a 'Longhouse Hilton' was under construction on a lake about forty minutes by boat from the village. This will mean the arrival of many more visitors who want to see the tribal peoples and their villages but who do not want to endure the 'hardship' of a night in a longhouse. As there is little for 'conventional' tourists to do apart from visit the longhouses and fish or do watersports on the lake, it is likely that the average duration of stay will only be two or three nights, resulting in a rapid turnover of visitors.

This sort of development raises some awkward questions concerning the desirability of tourist development. It is tempting to argue that such development should be stopped to protect local people and their cultures. But this is to argue that tribal peoples should remain 'untouched' in undeveloped 'reserves' for their protection and for our enjoyment. They themselves, quite understandably, do not wish to remain as a relict culture, immune from western development and prosperity. But tourism will undoubtedly destroy, or certainly modify, their traditional cultures. On the other hand, the dancer at the dance centre we spoke to argued that young people are already leaving villages for the towns, and that tourism, paradoxically, could help to save aspects of traditional culture under threat from development processes in general.

2.3 Kauai: turning back the clock

The third, and final, part of the programme, goes back to the Hawaiian Island of Kauai. The focus here is an attempt by the local people to regain a greater degree of control over the tourist industry in the wake of Hurricane Iniki which devastated large parts of the island's infrastructure. The native Hawaiians argue that the long-term future of the Hawaiian tourist industry rests on the culture of the Islands. Destroy the culture and you destroy the reasons why tourists come to Hawaii; only by preserving authentic Hawaiian culture will it be possible to maintain the tourist industry in the long term. Essentially the issue is the classic one of not destroying the goose that lays the golden egg. A similar issue will have to be faced in Sarawak and Malaysia.

Activities

Before the programme

Ideally, you should have read Chapter 5, 'Consuming spaces: global tourism', before the programme.

During the programme

There are three main points you should bear in mind as you watch the programme. The first is the expanding frontier of global tourism: what is untouched today may be a mass resort in twenty years. The second is the cultural impact of the tourist industry: what does tourism do to host societies? The final point is the uneven social relations of tourism: what is the impact of wealthy western visitors on local society and economy?

After the programme

Reflect on the issues raised during the programme. Is it possible or desirable for the scale and impact of tourism to be controlled, and is it inevitable that most benefits of tourist development will accrue to outside interests? Is it desirable for local people to control or have a say in the industry and is this likely to moderate or ameliorate some of the negative side-effects of tourist development?

TV5 'Alaska: the last frontier?'

Academic consultant: Philip Sarre

Producer: Eleanor Morris

1 Aims/links

This programme relates to Volume 3 Chapter 1, using material filmed in Alaska to develop section 1.2.2 and especially to contrast white American views of Alaska as empty wilderness with the reality of native Alaskan history and experience.

The programme also raises additional issues not directly addressed in the chapter:

o   How can the past settlement and use of apparently wild areas be recognized and reconstructed – especially in areas that have been 'emptied'?

o   What is it like to grow up as a member of a native group – especially when that group is treated as if 'invisible'?

o   How can native attitudes and practices influence land management for recreational purposes?

2 The programme

The issues at the heart of the programme begin to come alive with an interview with Don Followes, formerly of the National Parks Service and leader of the team which established the Kenai Fjords National Park (see Figure 5). He shows that the way the area was represented was crucial in persuading the US Congress and the local population to accept the National Park. His representation was explicitly designed to fit tourist demand. His assumption throughout was that the area was empty: 'nobody went there'.

The programme goes on to show that this apparent emptiness was illusory. Aron Crowell, an archaeologist at the University of California, describes how he has investigated former village sites in the Kenai Fjords and established hundreds of years of occupation by Yupik Eskimo groups. He refers to the discovery of over 2,000 such sites along this stretch of coast by teams involved in the clean-up of oil pollution from the *Exxon Valdez*. The evidence shows that the area was occupied as soon as the retreat of the glaciers permitted, and up until the nineteenth century.

The second stage of reconstructing the history of the Kenai Fjords follows Linda Cook, a historian working for the National Park Service in Anchorage, on a visit to a Chugach* Eskimo village west of Kenai Fjords. She describes how historical records from the Russian period and census records from 1891 confirm widespread native settlement and use of the

---

*Eskimos fall into two language groups: the Inuit, the largest group, in northern Alaska and Canada and the Yupik in southern Alaska. The Chugach are a subdivision of the Yupik Eskimos, living in Cook Inlet, Kenai and Prince William Sound.

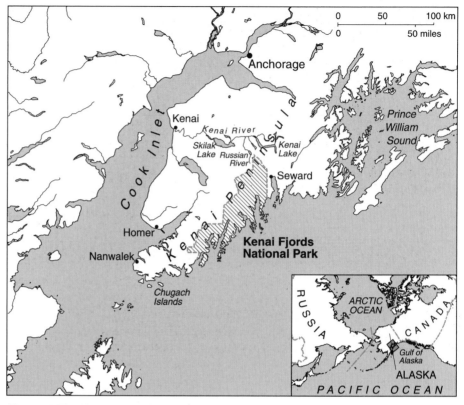

Figure 5 *The Kenai Peninsula, Alaska*

coast. She alludes to population decline as a result of disease, but emphasizes the role of Russian Orthodox priests in concentrating Eskimos into a few settlements, including the one we visit. The name of the settlement mirrors its history: originally Nanwalek, then Alexandrovsk, then English Bay, now once more Nanwalek. Linda Cook describes the slow process of using the oral tradition to reconstruct the history of the native people, which was largely omitted from histories based on written records produced by the white visitors.

Nanwalek is an isolated settlement where native groups have maintained some cohesion, so the focus of the programme moves to the valley of the Kenai River to examine the experience of the Denaina people who lived in the area, the Kenaitse. Their historic experience was to have their hunting land urbanized and their subsistence fishing pushed out by a combination of commercial fishing for the salmon canneries and sport fishing by growing numbers of tourists flocking to the Kenai and Russian Rivers. In July, when thousands of anglers crowd the banks of these rivers in pursuit of 100-pound king salmon, the result is known as 'combat fishing', with damage to the river environment and scant regard for other users of the land.

The accounts given by Kenaitse people show that their experience has been one of collective and individual invisibility, until the last few years, as their land was settled, and their only role was to provide casual labour in the fishery. For some, invisibility was chosen as they were blond and blue-eyed as a result of interbreeding with Scandinavians who came to the area

Airport terminal building, Nanwalek. Light aircraft are the main link between Nanwalek and Homer, the nearest town

during the Russian period. The strongest source of coherence for these people was the Russian Orthodox church, but some left the community to 'pass' as white, while others succumbed to drink and drugs.

Recent years have seen a resurgence of the community, both culturally and politically. Much of this is owed to outstanding people: Peter Kalifornski collected and published Denaina stories and attracted anthropological interest, as well as inspiring a revival in language and dance; and Clare Swann, the current tribal chief, has led political and legal challenges to re-establish rights to subsistence fishing and to administer welfare programmes. Unlike other native Alaskans, who benefited from land and financial awards in the Alaska Native Claims Settlement Act of 1971, the Kenaitse were not recognized nor awarded land. Their current position is very much a result of their own efforts.

The final section of the programme looks at a development which shows how the Denaina traditions and their current reputation have contributed to improved land and water management. It shows how the US Forest Service has worked with the Kenaitse, first to protect one of their past settlement sites from damage by boats and campers, and then to design an interpretative centre which will show how Denaina cultures used the natural resources of the area to sustain a culture and lifestyle which has low environmental impacts. Indeed, these low impacts were a key factor in allowing white people to see a wild and empty land. Now the hope is to use Denaina beliefs and practices to influence white Americans towards more sustainable lifestyles.

Kenaitse dance group. Reviving traditional dance is one of the ways in which young people are encouraged to take a positive view of being native Alaskans

Activities

Before the programme

Make sure that you have read at least Volume 3 Chapter 1, section 1.2.2 and Reading A by Mark Nuttall. Note the issues the programme will address, as listed in section 1 of these notes.

During the programme

Keep alert for different representations of the Alaskan landscape expressed or implied by different speakers. What were the implications of those representations about who could use resources, and how?

After the programme

Answer the following questions:

1   What were the desirable features of Alaska for tourists in the 'lower 48'?

2   How did Don Followes use those expectations to 'package' his National Park proposal?

3   Aron Crowell explained that only special sites sheltered from the open sea and protected from avalanches were suitable for Eskimo settlement. How do you think this might relate to the growing use of the National Park for canoe tourism?

Not only is there a direct conflict when canoeists camp on archaeological sites, but a more formal conflict has arisen from awards under the Alaska Native Claims Settlement Act. The Act gave the Chugach Eskimos the title to small areas in the National Park which were of particular cultural significance to them: they chose village sites which are also the main canoeist landing places. When we visited Kenai, this issue was just coming to the surface.

When thinking about Nanwalek and the conflicting cultural pressures on young native Alaskans, think back to earlier examples in Mexico, Malaysia and Hawaii of local cultures reasserting themselves against global tourism and international cultural pressures. Are there lessons which these groups might share?

If the Kenaitse have to learn their own language in formal classes and depend on white anthropologists for most of their knowledge of their own culture, do you think that their views can be seen as authentic, and how should environmental managers treat them?

A persuasive answer to this question comes from Fred Clark near the end of the programme, when he comments that cultures are not static but constantly developing. The development is likely to be one-sided because the Kenaitse have little political power, but their cultural attitudes and practices, which involve a reverence for nature and promote sustainability through limitation of catches and recycling of remains, do seem to resonate with those of American environmentalists in some respects.

Finally, look again at Chapter 1, Reading A by Nuttall to remind yourself of areas where Eskimo practices contradict those of American and European environmentalists. You might also ask yourself how you personally respond to the notion of sustainable yields of sea otter pelts.

TV6 'Population transition in Italy'

Academic consultant: Philip Sarre

Producer: Jack Leathem

1 Aims/links

This programme follows up one of the crucial issues in understanding population change in an area established by Volume 3 Chapter 3 as an extreme case: Italy. The issue is fertility decline – the key process which has stopped periods of rapid population growth in many countries during the twentieth century. Italy is an extreme case both in terms of the speed of the decline – from one of Europe's higher birth rates in 1965 to the lowest in 1980 – and in terms of the record low levels achieved. A decade ago demographers saw 'zero population growth' – implying a long-term fertility rate of two children per woman – as the lowest level imaginable. Italy as a whole currently has an average of 1.3 children per woman – and Liguria and Emilia Romagna have an average of only 0.9. Even the Mezzogiorno (the south of Italy), the source of Italy's reputation as the land of the large family, has a rate of about 1.6, less than those of France or Britain. (See Figure 6.)

The comparisons above make a point which you should bear in mind while watching the programme: namely, that fertility rates are uneven within and between countries as well as between continents. These variations are both a warning against overgeneralization and helpful in assessing the effects of particular factors and combinations of factors. The explanation which emerges from the programme is one which combines many factors, some in surprising ways.

2 The programme

The opening sequence states the question the programme addresses: how has Italy, known as a country of high birth rates and mass emigration, come, by the early 1990s, to be the country with the lowest fertility?

Two of Italy's leading demographers start by describing what has happened to Italy's demographic regime. Professor Antonio Golini stresses that, in spite of high life expectancy, current levels of fertility would reduce Italy's population by 60 per cent if continued for a century. Valerio Terra-Abrami, of ISTAT, explains the regional differences and points out that northern Italy has had low fertility for many years, but that this was obscured by high fertility in the south and migration from south to north. However, all areas have seen further falls in fertility since 1965.

Armando Montanari stresses the similarities between Italy's experience and that of other countries in Europe. The common pattern has been for industrialization and urbanization to bring about a process of 'demographic transition', ending with low death and birth rates and a stable population. In this respect, Italy only differs from northern Europe in industrializing later, mainly since the Second World War, and very rapidly. This seems to explain the rapidity of demographic change but not its extremely low fertility. The lateness of the industrialization has made

Figure 6 The regions of Italy

Italians very aware of women's move from being home-makers to employment, and many identify this as a key explanation of low fertility. However, women's employment is much less common in Italy than in Scandinavia where fertility is higher.

One possible explanation is that, because Italy industrialized late, it missed the experience of low unemployment and high economic growth elsewhere in Europe in the 1960s and the consequent development of elaborate urban infrastructure and welfare systems. These systems seem to underpin recent increases in fertility in countries like Germany and

Sweden, so it seems possible that their absence exerts an overall influence in Italy. The interview with Susanna Carella shows that Italian parents lack this support.

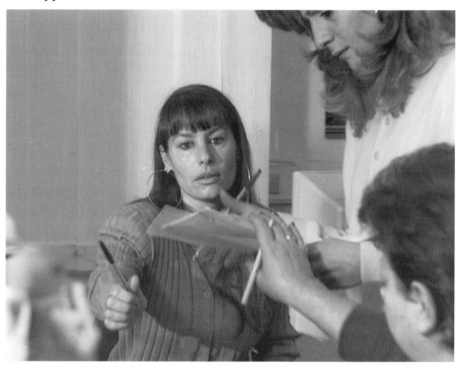

Susanna Carella at her place of work

The problem with this explanation is that the region of Italy with the most extreme fertility decline – Emilia Romagna – is the region which, because it has been the heartland of communist local government, has the best social services in the country. The special influences which are found in the region are described by Professor Piero Dagradi of the University of Bologna and Marco Ricci of the local branch of ISTAT. Emilia Romagna is the heartland of a region and style of development known to geographers and economists as 'Third Italy'. It is neither the depressed rural economy of the south nor the mass production industrial area of the north-west. The Third Italy is characterized by many small firms working in fashion and/or high-tech industries in a highly flexible structure of employment and subcontracting. It has been the most dynamic sector of Italy for the last two decades and has achieved the highest living standards. Important factors in relation to population change are the flexibility, and hence insecurity, of employment and the strong emphasis on style in clothes, cars and lifestyle. The interview with Antonia Patuelli and Giorgio Bonoli makes clear the difficulty of fitting child-raising into this pattern of life.

Having raised questions about the role of culture in the form of stylish consumer culture, the programme returns to Rome to confront the central paradox of record low fertility in the heartland of Roman Catholicism. In the face of Papal insistence on the immorality of contraception and its commonly perceived role in sustaining fertility in the less developed world, how can we explain Italy's achievement of the lowest fertility ever recorded for a major population? Part of the explanation is negative: only a third of Italians claim to be practising Catholics, and Father Mario Picchi suggests that for many of them Catholicism was an outward form of social conformity rather than a deeply felt personal belief. As a result, most Italians have no problem in adopting contraception, at least since it became legal. The use of contraception is necessary to achieve low fertility, but once more this only puts Italians on a par with northern Europeans and does not explain the record low fertility.

The programme visits Rome to explore the central paradox of record low fertility in the heartland of Roman Catholicism

The final step in the argument of the programme is to point out that Catholic beliefs about personal conduct and high ideals of family life play a positive role in lowering fertility. Italian society still takes a very negative view of the cohabitation of unmarried people and childbearing outside marriage. Statistics confirm that these practices are still rare in Italy, whereas they are now very common in northern Europe. So, as well as fewer and later marriages, with careful calculation and restriction of childbearing, Italy has very few extramarital births. Paradoxically, the high ideals of family life seem to act to deter many Italians from accepting the more flexible and compromised kinds of relationship which Van de Kaa (1987) has characterized as the 'second demographic transition' of northern Europe.

Finally, it is noted that the programme's diagnosis of the crucial role of Catholic family values on top of late and rapid industrialization with restricted welfare systems is consistent with the fact that demographers expect Italy to be overtaken imminently as the country of record low fertility by an even more Catholic country – Spain.

Activities

Before the programme

Read the sections of Volume 3 Chapter 3 which analyse the rise and stabilization of Europe's population.

During the programme

Note the different strands of explanation put forward and assess how plausible you find them.

After the programme

Your main activity after viewing the programme should be to relate the strands of the explanation put forward to the wider analysis of European population growth and stabilization as given in Chapter 3. In doing so, focus on where trends occurred faster or slower and use spatial unevenness to test how the different combinations of factors interact.

Finally, reflect on the views of the speakers about the implications of low fertility for Italian society and the economy. Since Fascist times, Italian politicians have sought to avoid population policy, but a rapid decline in population, together with mass immigration and overall ageing, seems to make this an issue which cannot be avoided. Given the explanation outlined above, what do you think would be the best way of bringing Italy's population into a more balanced state?

Reference

VAN DE KAA, D. J. (1987) 'Europe's second demographic transition', *Population Bulletin*, Vol. 42, No. 1, pp. 1–57.

TV7 'Water is for fighting over'

Academic consultant: John Blunden

Producer: Jack Leathem

1 Aims/links

This programme links directly to Volume 3 Chapter 4, section 4.6, and the problems posed by a scarcity of water in areas where rainfall is insufficient to meet local/regional needs. Both Audiocassette 2, Side B, and this television programme provide additional depth to the discussion in the text, with the audiocassette looking at a less developed country and the extent to which there may be any justification for the imposition of large-scale water schemes if these cause massive disruption to the 'way of life' of rural communities. National versus local interests are therefore brought to the fore, as is the role of major global funding agencies in helping to promote schemes which may not only be culturally damaging, but also environmentally undesirable.

The television programme is also concerned with the impact of water resource developments on long-established indigenous peoples, although its aim is to consider, as well, the problems posed by water as a scarce shared resource in a developed country. The case study chosen is that of the Truckee–Carson Basin, an area which lies partly in the Sierra Nevada mountains of California, but largely in the semi-arid desert of the Great Basin of Nevada: see Figure 7. However, in the making of the programme,

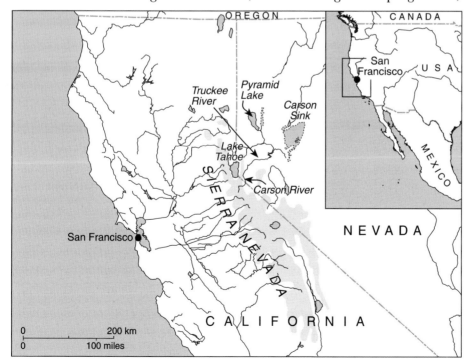

Figure 7   *Location of the Truckee–Carson Basin in the Sierra Nevada*

a more sophisticated sub-set of issues relevant to section 4.6 and Chapter 4 as a whole are considered. These include:

1   The complex interactions which can occur between a range of interest groups contesting their share of the water resources.

2   Inequalities in the bargaining positions of each of these groups, leading to:

3   The changing nature of their respective power bases and the reasons for this.

4   The extent to which consensus is achievable between the groups regarding the sharing of the resource.

5   Different perspectives regarding the future water prospects for each of the groups, including their own perception of likely changes in their needs.

6   The setting of the case study in a broader context, including that of the regional (where inter-state relationships become involved), the national (including federal interests) and the global.

The case study also touches on broader societal issues which are confrontational and have a global resonance, such as: urban expansion versus the preservation of agricultural land; unchecked development versus vanishing wetlands and open space; and western-style economic development versus the maintenance of traditional values.

2   The programme

The programme shows the setting of the case study – a drainage system which consists of two rivers which rise in the well-watered Sierra Nevada mountains, one at Lake Tahoe and the other in the mountains to the immediate south. Both flow eastwards down into the desert of the Great Basin of Nevada with the Truckee River terminating in the Pyramid Lake about 90 miles from its source and the Carson River in the Carson Sink about 110 miles from its source. (See Figure 8.)

The various interest groups are well-defined within the programme and include:

1   Truckee recreation interests in and around Lake Tahoe, including Truckee township and Stampede Reservoir at the head of the basin.

2   Westpac, suppliers of water to commercial and residential properties in Reno/Sparks and the Truckee Meadows along the Truckee River.

3   Pyramid Lake Paiute Indian Tribe in the reservation area, including Pyramid Lake (where the Truckee River ends), the Pyramid Lake fisheries and the irrigated farmland to the south of Pyramid Lake.

4   Truckee–Carson Irrigation District (TCID) and Newlands farmers who occupy the irrigated farmland of the Carson valley.

5   Fallon Paiute Indian Tribe – as (4) above, but with irrigated land in the reserve.

6   Wildlife and conservation at the Stillwater Natural Wildlife Refuge (part of the Carson Sink) and at Anaho Island in Pyramid Lake.

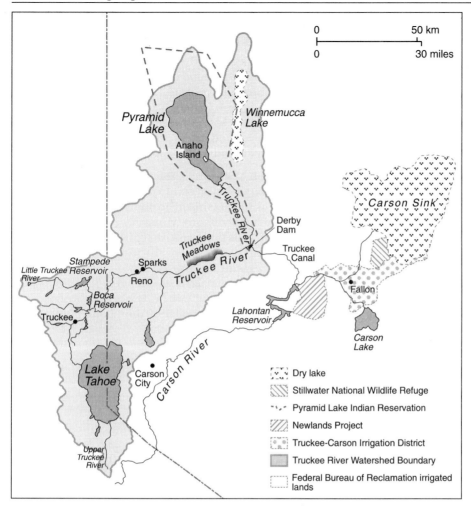

Figure 8 The Truckee–Carson Basin

Interviews with representatives of these groups:

o   provide a clear case for the water needs of their own interest group;

o   outline what their problems have been in the past with respect to achieving their water objectives;

o   explain whether these needs have been adequately met by the Negotiated Settlement Act when it comes into force in 1996;

o   outline the extent to which they see the Act as flexible enough to take account of changed needs in the future;

o   state whether they see their own interests as sustainable in the longer term when viewed against other legitimate claims, and the regional/national/global pressures for change.

Obviously, there are some variations in this basic approach. The TCID, for example, played no part in the realization of the Negotiated Settlement Act.

In the case of communities such as those of the native American peoples, the nature of their traditional lifestyles and the role of water in these is explored. Also, Newlands farmers expound the virtues of what they claim

Pyramid Lake Paiute native American children with some of the fish grown in the fisheries

as their traditional 'way of life', even though they are the descendants of families deliberately moved to the Carson Valley as a result of federal government policy in the early part of the twentieth century.

Finally, there remain the contributions to the programme of state and federal departments. The Federal Bureau of Reclamation is the body responsible for the development of the Newlands Project as part of a national irrigation programme aimed at establishing farming communities in underpopulated arid lands of the west; a representative explains this particular policy, its current legacy and future relevance. Representatives of the Departments of Water Resources (California) and Conservation and Natural Resources (Nevada) provide comments on water allocations between the two states involved, as well as a more detached overview of water conflicts. The latter involves an appraisal of the ways in which these conflicts have developed, and the role of the interest groups in preparing the way for the Negotiated Settlement Act. These agencies also comment on the significance of general changes of attitude towards minority groups such as the native American peoples, and towards environmental conservation in the achievement of the Act. In conclusion, they comment on the part likely to be played in the future by exogenous national and global forces acting upon interest groups in the Truckee–Carson Basin.

An example of the artificial fish-runs constructed to take the fish 'upstream' to spawn from the fisheries in Pyramid Lake. The obstacles are necessary to persuade the fish that they have reached their breeding area

Activities

Before the programme

Make sure that you have thoroughly understood the context of this programme by studying section 4.6 of Chapter 4 and listening to the associated Audiocassette 2, Side B.

During the programme

As you watch the programme, try to note the different attitudes to nature and 'natural resources' evident in the lifestyles of the different interest groups. What, apart from a shared consideration of water as a resource, is the common theme that underpins both the television programme and Audiocassette 2, Side B? Also, you may wish to think about why, in the context of the case studies of TV7 and the audiocassette, is conflict resolution a more likely outcome in the developed than in the developing country?

After the programme

You may find it useful to compare and contrast the extent to which indigenous peoples in the two media case studies relating to water resources have been able to effect favourable outcomes for themselves. To what extent might exogenous global factors still influence the 'negotiated settlement' achieved in the Truckee–Carson Basin?

TV8 'A migrant's heart'

Academic consultant: Steve Pile

Producer: Patti Langton

1   Aims/links

This programme takes its cue from the themes of migration, connections between disparate places, and senses of place found in Chapter 1 of Volume 4. At the outset of that chapter, Russell King cites a poem written on the 'emigrant's monument' to talk about the kinds of distances involved in migration. The monument can be found in La Coruña, Spain, and it looks out over the ocean towards far-off lands. There are three direct links between the programme and King's observations about this monument. *Firstly,* the connection King makes here is Imperial. Thus, the 'emigrant's monument' commemorates the migrations to Central and South America which were set up within the context of Spain's military conquest and economic exploitation of its colonies in those regions. *Secondly,* the Gallego poem, for King, speaks of the 'multitude of human dramas and feelings' which lay within colonial migrations. Moreover, bound up in migrations are senses of place: the migrant's heart is spread over land and sea, irrevocably altering their senses of place. *Lastly,* King points out that there are many stories in migration and that it is difficult to convey the pain of departure and the deep homesickness that can result from saying goodbye to a familiar landscape, to one's birthplace, home and village. Thus, the poignancy of the poem lies partly in the sentiment that the migrant will never return.

The aim of this programme is to explore the kinds of feelings about migration and displacement which migrants have. King explains that 'migrants engage with place in several ways' and, in this programme, one migrant reveals how the meaning of places is indelible – even for a migrant without roots. The central figure in the programme is Jatinder Verma. Through a journey to specific places in India and England which have particular – often symbolic – meaning for him as a migrant, he traces out the displacements and ambivalences associated with his situation. Before moving on, take a little time to think about what displacement and ambivalence might mean for the migrant. In this context, King describes the ways in which the migrant's sense of place and of personal identity often involve a duality of 'here' and 'there' (see section 1.5 of Chapter 1). This experience can be unsettling for someone who had roots in their home-place, but Jatinder has always had to live within a displaced migrant's world.

The main links of the programme can be teased out from King's discussion of the 'emigrant's monument'. *First,* it is important not to underestimate the importance of distance and changes in such spatial relationships. Distance may stretch personal relationships to breaking-point. On the other hand, it may enable people to gain a perspective on things that they would not otherwise have had. Thus, for example, it is useful to think about why the poem on the Spanish monument tells of the emigrant's departure, but not of their return. *Secondly,* the ghost in every place presented in this programme is Imperialism and the history of its arrival, establishment, collapse and departure. Imperialism is not just associated with European states: the Mughal (commonly spelt Mogul) Emperors built their capitals, palaces and tombs in India too, for example. Nevertheless, it is the migrations associated with the British Empire, and after, which are the focus of this programme – though you will see that these take very different forms. As King says, there is a multitude of human dramas in every colonial and post-colonial situation, but this does not mean that successive imperial projects have similar effects. *Lastly,* the drama of migration involves people who feel: people who feel about places and for whom places provide meaning. The experience of migration and senses of place are bound up one in the other, but there are as many ways in which this can work out as there are migrants. In this respect, the duality of 'here' and 'there' plays out in distinct ways for Jatinder: for example, he can claim all of 'India' as a meaningful place simply because he was not born 'there' and is therefore not from a specific place or district *in* India.

This programme reveals something about one migrant's heart, but this heart does not have one story or one feeling, but different stories and different feelings. There is no one story in the migrant's sense of place, there are always the ghosts of other stories.

2 The programme

2.1 Introduction: Jatinder Verma and Tara Arts Group

For this programme, we asked Jatinder Verma to provide a visual essay on his experience of migration and his senses of different places, not only because he himself is a migrant and because of his, his family's and his friends' experiences of migration, but also because his personal journey resonates so strongly with the themes of Chapter 1.

Jatinder was brought up in Nairobi, British East Africa (now Kenya). His parents are both Punjabi, whose migration from India was made possible by the links between the two continents created by the British Empire. In section 1.2 of his chapter, King notes that over 30 million people were extracted from the Indian subcontinent by the British colonial authorities. Jatinder's father was one of these people. Almost typically, he was shipped out from Bombay to work on a railway-building project in East Africa, where he eventually became a station-master. As the son of Indians in a British African colonial context, he was brought up speaking Hindi and Swahili, English and French, and Punjabi. In one sense, his privilege is that he can move freely between these languages, each giving him access to different cultures and sensibilities. On the other hand, he is never free to speak these languages as his own because Jatinder now lives in England. If, as Salman Rushdie astutely observes, the trouble with Britain is that its history happened abroad, then in one sense at least that history has come home. But this is not a happy ending, nor an end to history, because Jatinder remains a displaced person. This displacement can be found in at least three dimensions: Kenya was home, but Jatinder is Indian; he is an Indian, but he was not brought up there; England is the mother country and he *is* British, but he is not white. Jatinder is perpetually caught in an incessant oscillation between 'here' and 'there', wherever he is, because he can never claim to be (at) home or to have returned to his roots.

Jatinder is, at the time of writing, the artistic director of Tara Arts, which is the foremost Asian theatre company in Britain. He has written plays and his success has made him well-known, so much so that he is one of the subject's of Pratibha Parmar's film, *The Colour of Britain* (1994). His work traffics between Eastern and Western art traditions, simultaneously challenging what it means to be British and also creating an exciting new *British* theatre, which Jatinder calls 'Binglish'. Indeed, it is possible to think of this distinctive theatre language as an expression of what King refers to as cultural hybridity (an example is given below). Further, it is an example of the ways in which King says migrants transform urban space to resemble and voice their experiences (see section 1.5 of Chapter 1): in Jatinder's case, it is a public theatre space in South London.

Jatinder regularly visits India, especially New Delhi, and works in close relation with Indian artists.

2.2 Jatinder's journey

> *humm wahaan hain jahaan se humm ko bhi*
> *Kuchh hummaari khaburr nahin aati*

> *I am in that oblivious state*
> *A stranger to myself where I am*

These words were written by the nineteenth-century Urdu poet, Mirza Ghalib. They are also particularly meaningful for Jatinder because they say so much about his migrant's heart. More than this, it says something about the orientation of his feelings towards places. It tells of estrangement and alienation. While migration may sometimes produce an alienated heart, the migrant's senses of place are not solely defined by estrangement. In this programme, Jatinder takes us on a journey to specific sites in New Delhi, Punjab and London which have particular meanings for him. Each place evokes different feelings within him, though these senses of place do not always point in the same direction. Each place has specific meanings for Jatinder, but these meanings sometimes clash head on. These sites are fragments of a migrant's heart. They are a collection of short stories about the duality, or double-sidedness, of his experience: on the one hand being in place, on the other hand feeling out of place; on the one hand being fixed in place, on the other being mobile between places.

This programme is not simply an account of a journey nor a collection of his sentiments about particular places, but an amalgam of both. In one sense at least, this programme plays on the relationship between routes: it is both Jatinder's journey (routes) and Jatinder's sense of displacement and emplacement in the world (roots). We can pull out these threads by looking at some of the places visited in the programme. [Please note: the order in which we deal with these places in these notes differs slightly from the sequence of the programme.]

Given the importance to Jatinder of the lines of Urdu poetry cited above, one of the last sites he visits before returning to England is Mirza Ghalib's tomb in the Nizamuddin neighbourhood of south Delhi. Before this he

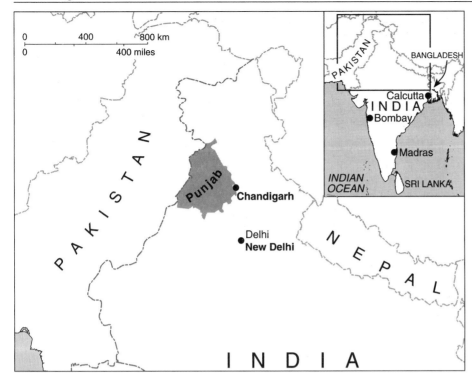

Figure 9   *India, showing the location of the cities of New Delhi and Chandigarh, and the district of the Punjab*

goes to places which stir up strong emotions for him and which, thereby, act as sites where he can think about his relationship to India and Indian arts. You will see him in these places and hear his thoughts and feelings about them as we recorded them at the time. It is useful to provide some background information which helps us understand the links between Jatinder's experiences of migration and his senses of place. In particular, the connection is imperial.

In terms of this part of the course, two particularly important sites are Humayun's tomb and the Lal-Qila (usually translated as 'The Red Fort') because they embody colonial encounters – between a Mughal Empire and an ascendant British Empire. Here is some background as provided by the Indian Archaeological Survey (quotes are taken from unpublished sources):

(a) *Humayun's tomb* was 'built in 1565 by Humayun's widow Bega Begam [and mother of Akbar] nine years after her husband's death. It is the first substantial example of the Mughal architecture, with octagonal plan, lofty arches, pillared kiosks and double dome, which occurs here for the first time in India ... [and] ... which culminated in the Taj Mahal at Agra... It was in this tomb in 1857 that Bahadur Shah II, the last Mughal Emperor of Delhi, had taken shelter with his sons and was captured by Lt Hodson.'

(b) *Lal-Qila* was 'built by the Mughal Emperor Shah Jahan as royal residence within his new capital of shahjahanabad [Old Delhi], the Lal-Qila (Red Fort) has a perimeter of 2.41km ... The two famous architects Ustad

Jatinder is filmed 'contemplating' at Humayun's tomb. This sequence was dropped from the final programme

Hamid and Ustad Ahmed were associated with the construction which took nine years (AD 1639–48) for completion.'

For Jatinder, these two sites reveal a history of successive invasions of northern India by peoples from eastern Europe and central Asia, but especially their settlement by two invading Empires – the Mughal and the British. Jatinder points to the similarities and differences of Mughal and British settlement. Although the first British emissaries (travelling during Elizabeth I's reign) were received at Humayun's tomb with respect, Jatinder argues, they were not invited to reduce the Mughal Emperors to puppet kings. Another key difference, for Jatinder, is that the Mughals came to India to stay. They built their tombs, mosques, palaces and capitals in the region, while the British remained invaders from outside – their graves, churches, residences and administrative centres were never more than colonial expediencies. Moreover, the beginning of the British Raj (1857–1947) was marked by the brutal suppression of the First War of Independence in 1857 (commonly known in Britain as the Indian Mutiny). The British finally capturing the so-called mutineer, Bahadur Shah, at the Lal-Qila after a long and bloody siege. The legacy of British colonial administration is still traced through Indian society some fifty years after Independence in 1947. For example, today, the Lal-Qila and the Viceroy's Palace remain key symbolic sites for official ceremonies in Indian political life, while English is the language of the élite and the polity.

For Jatinder, the area around the Lal-Qila (Red Fort) juxtaposes three key elements of Indian life. Sited on nearby high ground is the largest mosque of India, Jami Masjid, built between 1644 and 1656. Between the mosque and Lal-Qila is Chandni Chowk (literally Silver Courtyard). Jatinder is particularly struck not only by the close proximity of these three places, but also by the way each symbolizes a different form of

Filming Jatinder's piece 'to camera' at Lal-Qila, the Red Fort

power: of the state, of religion and of the market. In TV1, Doreen Massey pointed out the juxtaposition in the Mexican village, Acancéh, of a Catholic Church, an ancient Mayan pyramid and a modern-day market. Similarly, in Old Delhi, we find the heart of military power, Lal-Qila, overlooked by the focal point of religious power, Jami Masjid, surrounded by the encroaching market, Chandni Chowk.

Chandni Chowk is the major bazaar area of Old Delhi and consists of a labyrinth of narrow side-streets, each with its own bustling market – and it is here that Jatinder meets Sonia, his sister's daughter, who is visiting India for the first time. Chandni Chowk is not, however, randomly organized. *Firstly*, it is organized by commodity: certain streets specialize in, for example, spices while in others can be found silver merchants, clothiers and 'secondhand' goods traders. Less obviously, *secondly*, the area is divided along religious lines: Muslim and Hindu businesses are not found side-by-side. In general, Hindu shops are found on the major shopping roads, while Muslim businesses are found in the streets behind. Chandni Chowk is a site where many people from different places come to bargain and exchange, but it is also a site of conflict – occasionally, but especially on Fridays, when Muslims come to pray in the mosque, there are running battles between Muslims and Hindus in the streets.

Jatinder visits another site, Jantar Mantar, where the juxtaposition of different constructions is a testament to a history of migrations and changing relationships between the East and the West. (You may find it interesting to compare and contrast this observatory with the Mayan cosmology and geographical imagination shown in TV1.) The Indian Archaeological Survey describes Jantar Mantar as 'an observatory consisting of masonry-built astronomical instruments, erected by Maharaja Jai Singh II of Jaipur (AD 1699–1743). He was keenly interested in astronomical observations and studied all known systems Eastern and Western, before embarking on this construction at Delhi [about AD 1724]

... The instruments are built of brick and rubble, plastered with lime and bear graduated markings to take readings.' One instrument, Misra Yantra, which looks a bit like a butterfly, is 'a composite instrument; indicating the meridian (noon) at four places, two in Europe, one each in Japan and the Pacific Ocean.' You might want to ask yourself why the Maharaja wanted to know when it was noon in Europe and the Pacific Rim.

You can also see, behind Misra Yantra, contrasting modern buildings – the instruments of the calculus of international capital. Jatinder argues that, while Jantar Mantar is a site of mutual exchange between different kinds of science which are sensitive to local conditions, whose reach extends from Europe to the Pacific to the stars and the zodiac, the office and tower blocks symbolize the invasion of a form of exchange grounded in the cold rationality of capital accumulation, its insensitivities to local knowledge and its universalizing impulses.

In the programme there are two other places where Jatinder explores the duality of his feelings about displacement. *First*, the programme shows how Jatinder's travelling between England and India involves his work in the theatre. In particular, the Naqqal female impersonators are shown, though in two very different situations. Given that this is a popular art form, we might expect to see them playing before an audience of poor people in an informal setting. Initially, we see them performing in an ad hoc shrine, which is situated by the road which borders and separates the planned city of Chandigarh and an outer jhuggi (an informal settlement consisting of shacks). Less predictably, they are also part of an ensemble of players rehearsing *The Madwoman of Chaillot* in Punjabi which, coincidentally, at the time of first broadcast of TV8 (on 1 July 1995), was being performed at the Waterman's Art Centre in West London.

Secondly, we see Jatinder in London: travelling by train; at home; walking the dog; and at work during rehearsals of a production for the National Theatre in London – which involves a reinterpretation and mixing of stories involving noses, from the Hindu deity Ganesh to Pinocchio (this is an example of Jatinder's blending of distinctive cultural traditions into something different, 'Binglish'). On Waterloo Bridge Jatinder stops to think about the connections that the River Thames makes between the city – the heart of empire – and the seas and oceans that flow between other lands. Drawing on his Sanskrit scholarship, T. S. Eliot wrote these appropriate lines in his poem, *The Waste Land*:

> *Sweet Thames, run softly till I end my song,*
> *Sweet Thames, run softly, for I speak not loud or long.*

For Jatinder, the Thames is both a root, a place which runs softly through until the end of the song, and a route, which runs sweetly to distant places.

These, then, are the 'roots' of Jatinder's experience of migration, his connections across the globe and his senses of place and identity. The roots are connected by routes, but Jatinder's displacement – as King's analysis of international migration suggests – raises important questions about the changing nature of 'place'.

2.3   Conclusion: migration, globalization and place

In Chapter 1 Russell King stresses three aspects of migration: first, that it is linked to processes of globalization; secondly, that it is both a product and a cause of uneven development between places; and, thirdly, that it raises important questions about the constitution of 'place'. For individual migrants, King suggests, displacement poses problems of identity: where is the migrant's place in the world?

King's analysis concentrates primarily on international movements of labour and the different conditions under which people move, whether they are slaves or guestworkers. Jatinder's connections and experiences add further aspects to this story. King argues that migration is becoming globalized: that is, that more and more countries are being integrated into a global migration system. Without contradicting this conclusion, this programme shows that this process is itself uneven: Jatinder's parents were moved through a particular integrating migration system – the British Empire – which was simultaneously, and in specific ways, local and global but which no longer exists as such. Although the legacy of Empire still impinges on migration, its demise has led to the disintegration of this particular local–global migration system. As King shows in his chapter, there is an uneven history and geography of migration and globalization where links are constantly being created and dissolved, where barriers to migration are perpetually being put up and taken down. Moreover, changing technology does not necessarily produce an increasingly integrated world migration system. The jet airliner allows Jatinder to visit India regularly, but the simple fact of being able to fly to India in ten hours does not make it easier to settle there.

This programme also suggests that migration is not solely based on the expediencies of the global economy and the local requirement for cheap labour power: there are also cultural factors involved. For example, the Naqqals moved across the border from Pakistan to India at the time of Partition (1947), not because of the need in India for female impersonators, but because of their religion. At the time of partition, Muslims moved to Pakistan while Hindus migrated in the opposite direction to India. Of course, Partition was itself a direct consequence of the British Empire. Jatinder's own work in the theatre does not imply that his migration is solely the deathly consequence of the modern imperialism of international economic empires, driven by the cold-hearted need to accumulate and circulate ever-increasing volumes of capital.

It is not merely an abstract theoretical point to state that Jatinder lives through the contradictions of both British imperialism and modern capitalism. At the beginning of these notes, it was suggested that Jatinder's experiences are saturated with feelings of displacement and ambivalence. It is appropriate to end with a comment or two about what this 'double-sidedness' means. The black psychoanalyst, critic and agitator Frantz Fanon talked about the ways in which the subjects of imperialism are involved in 'a grotesque psychodrama' where the colonized are forced to recognize and abide by the values of the colonizers (see Fanon, 1952). In this situation, the colonized are not allowed a valued place for their own beliefs and social practices. In many ways, the migrant's situation is similar: the migrant is forced to live within, and collude with, the morals and social practices of the host culture; the migrant is also cut off from the development of the value systems that have been left behind. For the migrant, there is literally no place like home. Living through the contradictions of movement and distance may provide opportunities which non-migrants can never have – a chance to reflect, maybe; on the other hand, the migrant's heart is shadowed by memories that become increasingly homeless.

Activities

Before the programme

Ideally, you should have read Chapter 1, 'Migrations, globalization and place', before you view the programme. In particular, sections 1.2 and 1.5 of Chapter 1 contain necessary background material.

During the programme

List the people Jatinder Verma meets in this programme and note their links to specific places – not forgetting Jatinder himself.

There are two broad aspects of migration which you should think about as you watch this programme:

(a) the ways in which particular places offer contradictory feelings about displacement for migrants at any one time – often depending upon their experiences of, and the meanings surrounding, both the place they are in and its social context;

(b) the particular ways in which social, personal and family relationships are stretched over space and time, noting especially how this plays out differently for the individuals presented in the programme.

After the programme

Using your list of characters and the places associated with them, spend some time putting down on paper their relation to the following:

o   Why have people, or people close to them, become involved in *migration*?

o   What does migration mean for the migrant's *sense of place*?

o   How important has *colonialism* been for the migrants in the programme? In what ways does racism figure in the migrants' experiences? What changes do you anticipate in this situation?

o   Would you say that people have been *forced to move* or not? Whether or not you think they have been forced to migrate, think about why you have made your choices. What do you understand by force in this context?

o   Is migration always a bad experience for the migrant? What are the positive aspects of migration – both for the migrant and the sites of in-migration?

At the outset of this course, we learnt that different maps of the world belie different geographical imaginations (in Chapter 1 of Volume 1 and also TV1). Moreover, it can be argued that maps are not just produced by cartography, but also by writing and imagining. If these arguments are plausible, then certain problems start to become apparent. In the context of thinking about the production of images about the experiences of migration, you might wish to consider the following questions:

o   What kinds of geographical imagination are used in the programme to convey Jatinder's experiences of migration, his senses of place and identity?

o   How far does the programme rely on familiar images of England and Englishness, and India and Indianness?

o   As a representation of Jatinder's experience of geography, in what ways might the programme filter out elements of his experience of migration, place and identity?

Reference

FANON, F. (1952) *Black Skin, White Masks*, London, Pluto Press.

TV9   'Who belongs to Glasgow?'

Academic consultant: Pat Jess

Producer: Jack Leathem

1   Aims/links

Two key ideas underpin this programme:

o   There are many different ways of interpreting and representing the character and identity of a place – many different geographical imaginations (remember Volume 1 Chapter 1 and TV1).

o   'Identities of places are a product of social action and of how people construct their own representations of particular places' (Volume 4 Chapter 4, section 4.1).

The programme aims:

(a) To explore ideas about place and identity using our concept of 'geographical imagination'.

(b) To do this by examining the *images* that represent a place, to reveal:

    (i)   how those images came about;

    (ii) two sets of relationships which are important in understanding the character of a place: power relations and local–global relations.

The programme was made in Glasgow in 1993. It is not about Glasgow as such: it is about Glasgow's *image*. It could have been made almost anywhere, so look at your own town or other places that you know, as further examples.

The programme is central to Volume 4 and links directly with Chapters 2 and 3. It also links with Volume 1 (Chapters 1 and 2) and TV1.

2   The programme

The programme is about *images*. Images are representations of places; they are constructed and contested. Images also represent multiple identities, uniqueness of place, interdependencies.

2.1   Why Glasgow?

Glasgow fulfils our aims and is also an interesting case study having, arguably, been the most successful among British cities in developing/ manufacturing a new identity in the 'post-industrial' era. Glasgow illustrates:

(a) power relations, reflected in:

o   constructed images – 'Glasgow's miles better' was a deliberate campaign to improve the image of Glasgow.

o   contested images – 'City of Culture' – but whose culture?

o   multiple identities – 'Clydebuilt', 'Red Clydeside', 'Shock City', 'Glasgow's Alive' are all images of Glasgow.

o   whose interests these dominant images represent and whose are ignored.

(b) local–global relations – phrases like 'second city of Empire' and 'a great European city' reflect how Glasgow's (local) uniqueness has been constructed out of wider (global) interdependence.

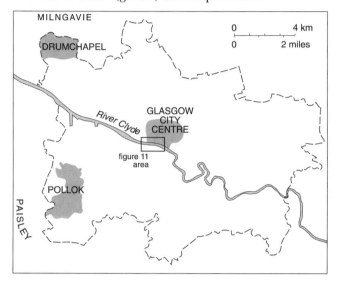

Figure 10   Glasgow

2.2   Background to the programme

Prior to its currently projected image of dynamism, Glasgow was regarded as the place which best illustrated all that was wrong with the modern industrial city: 'Once called the "second city of the British Empire", because of its size and industrial might, Glasgow had sunk so low that even the locals disdained it' (Bryson, 1989).

Glasgow's industrial base was laid during the latter half of the nineteenth century when the city became a prominent industrial centre. The idea of 'Clydebuilt' serves to illustrate the importance of the city in equipping, not only Britain itself, but also the far-flung reaches of the Empire with the ships, locomotives and heavy engineering commodities necessary to fuel economic expansion. Crucially, then, Glasgow's ('local') economic fortunes, as with those of many of the other 'older' industrial centres of Britain such as Tyneside and Belfast, were integrally tied to the ('global') fortunes of the British Empire. The saying 'Glasgow made the Clyde and the Clyde made Glasgow' highlights the importance of shipbuilding and, behind that, of trade for Glasgow's industrial growth in the nineteenth and early twentieth centuries. It also illustrates the theme of *interdependence* (Volume 4 Chapter 2, section 2.4.2). Industrial and economic decline in the period following the First World War, combined with growing problems of inadequate housing, rising unemployment and industrial agitation and militancy, gave rise to the image which arguably

has dominated reportage of Glasgow for most of this century. For example:

> There is something deeply wrong with the Clyde, ... that sends in repeated menace, to every successive Parliament, the same bitter group of extreme left members, irrespective of the changing political mood of the rest of the country, to kill with their fierce interruptions any restful optimism of the remainder of the House.
>
> (Bolitho, 1924)

This image, then, was a product of political agitation and conflict which had gripped much of Clydeside in the early part of this century. The period from around 1914 to the early 1920s, now known as 'The Red Clyde', was characterized by large-scale industrial conflict in the shipyards and factories. Community-based agitation over housing conditions gave rise to the 1915 rent strike which was organized mainly by women and received widespread support on Clydeside. Glasgow was regarded as a 'melting-pot' during the First World War when the government was increasingly concerned that a potentially revolutionary situation might develop. Glasgow during this period, then, was a very *political* place and this aspect of its history has also been reflected in many of the images and representations of the city over the decades.

Another image which developed during this period was that Glasgow was a very *violent* place. This is reflected in the novel *No Mean City*, written when the city was gripped by the inter-war slump and depression. This image and representation of Glasgow has dominated much of the discussion of the city ever since. It was reflected in the significant number

Glasgow's image as 'a very political place' – the Rent Strike of 1915 brought women into the local political arena

of novels, dramas, documentaries and television plays which highlighted Glasgow's 'hard side'. The work of Peter McDougall in the 1970s – an excerpt from which is included in the programme – serves to illustrate much of this negative image. But it is also claimed that this negative image of violence was constructed from outside the city by, among others, media based far away in London/England; it was essentially what others said about Glasgow. Glaswegians knew about these negative characteristics – and that they existed elsewhere as well – but they also knew other things about Glasgow which were never portrayed back to the outside world – that is, until the 'Glasgow's miles better' campaign was launched.

The image 'Glasgow's miles better' was deliberately constructed by the City Council, avowedly to make Glaswegians feel better about Glasgow but in fact largely on behalf of business. But it begged a question – 'miles better for whom?' Certainly, the city centre was better for shoppers and visitors and the new roads were literally 'miles better' for motorists but the spiralling problems of the housing schemes provided stark counter-images. In other words, as with all images, the image of 'miles better' was partial and selective. It was a particular, preferred representation. It excluded other aspects of the city. It was not promoting housing estates like Drumchapel, and they benefited either little or not at all. (See Volume 4 Chapter 3, sections 3.3.2 and 3.3.3, especially the explanation of the idea of 'the Other'.)

For many people, 1988 marked the arrival of Glasgow on the national scene in Britain, with the *National* Garden Festival (see Figure 11). For many Glaswegians it proved to be a missed opportunity to gain a lasting amenity, but for those promoting the city it was an important step. In 1990 Glasgow was *European* City of Culture. By the mid 1990s Glasgow was attracting *international* conferences (such as Rotary International in 1997 and City of Architecture and Design 1999). But the image of 'City of Culture' was particularly strongly contested. On the one hand Glasgow was looking outwards towards Europe in a new way – very different from the late nineteenth and the early part of the twentieth century. From another

glasgow
city of architecture
+ design
1999

The work of image-builders in constructing a new sense of place

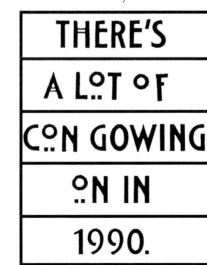

Contrasting images of Glasgow as European City of Culture in 1990: the official slogan, re-interpreted to highlight marginalized interests and concern over spending

perspective it was failing to look inwards: the promotion of European and international culture was accompanied by a denial and marginalization of Glasgow's own local culture. It was also argued that the city would be bankrupted in the process.

The economy of Glasgow has undergone a major transformation since the inter-war period. In common with many other 'old' industrial centres, the majority of the city's workforce is now engaged in service sector employment, a far cry from its image as an industrial city *par excellence*. In part this transition reflects Glasgow's changing position in both the national and international economies. (See Volume 4 Chapter 6, section 6.4.3.) In the 1980s substantial inward investment in the form of business services and tourist-related activities has further altered its traditional economic base (Volume 4 Chapter 2, section 2.4.3). Public and private sector agencies have been to the fore in promoting the city as a place in which to invest and the dominant image of Glasgow is a much more 'positive' one. From being a city characterized by violence and conflict, Glasgow is now marketed by the Glasgow Development Agency's Business Location Service as 'no mean city' in which to do business. This demonstrates that the same image can provide different interpretations, in this case one negative and one positive. It also serves to reinforce the point that images are built up over time, providing layers of representations. Contrasting images also illustrate the point that at any one time, more than one image or representation will be available. These alternative images frequently conflict with each other and, in different ways, refer to particular readings of previous histories to portray their messages, some of which may be hidden. (See also Volume 4 Chapter 4, section 4.2.)

Today's competing images, then, not only compete in relation to contemporary developments and future plans, but also compete in the interpretations of the past of a city such as Glasgow. In Glasgow today, images of a vibrant, modern *place*, as reflected in the idea of Merchant City, clearly invoke a particular sense of the past. In this respect Merchant City is a particular representation of Glasgow today and one that serves to exclude other images and representations. These contrast strongly with the images of the city's large peripheral housing estates, typified by Drumchapel, which are clearly the product of a very different social and historical context. We can see in this, examples of different 'envelopes of space–time', different geographical imaginations. (This idea is further developed in Volume 4 Chapter 4 and in Audiocassette 3 Side A.) While people in Glasgow often identify with the city itself, different localities within, and competing images of, the city will give rise to different ideas or 'senses' of place. Identifying with Drumchapel as opposed to Merchant City or with the city as a whole reinforces the point that *senses of place* operate at a number of different levels and spatial scales, which may contradict or compete with each other. While spatial or geographical scale clearly refers to identification with particular geographical entities, by 'different levels' we refer to the very different class and power relations involved in identifying with a place (Volume 4 Chapter 3, sections 3.3.2 and 3.3.3, and Audiocassette 3 Side A). It is clear that 'place' means different things to different social groups. There are different representations of place at work at any given time, giving rise to competing or contradictory identities with the same place. These, in turn, give rise to counter-claims that the 'real' Glasgow is not reflected in

GLASGOW

Every year we spend millions to attract your business.

NO MEAN

But we invest it wisely.

CITY

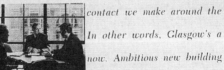

Glasgow is looking to a future full of opportunity, optimism and challenge. In other words, a future that's great for business. And today, Glasgow's energy, commitment and determination are bringing that future to life. Every penny of the millions we invest, every minute of the years of planning and thought, every handshake with every contact we make around the world brings it more into focus. In other words, Glasgow's a great place to do business right now. Ambitious new building projects, international communications, more training in new skills. Our investment has opened up a future full of opportunity for any business with the ambition to match Glasgow's. Come and see how your future looks in Glasgow, and watch it come alive. Because Glasgow is different, Glasgow's on the move, **Glasgow's Alive.**

Contact Stephen Running at the Business Location Service on 041-242 8400.

Turning an image around – new use for an old slogan, confronting Glasgow's reputation as a violent place

'Dual City' – different ways of imagining Glasgow (Drumchapel, above, and Merchant City, below)

Merchant City but in places like the peripheral estates. One of the dominant images to emerge from Glasgow in recent years, then, is the notion of a 'dual city': two cities experiencing very different social and economic fortunes in recent decades (see opposite).

2.3 How the programme progresses

The programme takes the form of a visit to Glasgow. We talked to people and asked about their image(s) of Glasgow and whether these had changed – what was the 'old' image; what is the 'new'; how has it changed; what will it be like in another ten years?

The five main participants have different experiences of Glasgow and these are represented in the images which they hold and aspects of the city's character which they highlight. The themes and ideas behind the programme are all to be found in what they say and what they see.

Gordon Borthwick talks about the long history of Glasgow and denies its violent image as being worse than elsewhere. His perspective highlights what he sees as the city's *heritage* which links the past with the present and the future.

Linda Whiteford is part of the city's positive image-building. She sees a place that has always been better than it was painted and sees it now in a very positive, vibrant light.

Jean Forbes sees the urban regeneration process as positive and expects the benefits to 'trickle down' to other parts of the city – while acknowledging that this process has been slowed by recession in the economy.

Gerry Mooney points out many of the contrasts in Glasgow's image, or images, and adopts a more critical stance. He discusses the key concepts and themes which provide the framework for the programme.

Edward Stephenson looks, above all, to locality (Drumchapel) rather than to city or region. But he identifies *with* Glasgow *against* Belfast, London or Edinburgh.

Postscript

A headline-grabbing weekend of 'midsummer madness', when six murders occurred in (parts of) Glasgow over the weekend of 5–6 August 1995, reinforced the ongoing nature of contestation and debate about the issues discussed in the programme. As noted in *The Scotsman* (8 August 1995), the legacy of the imagery of *No Mean City* was quickly resurrected by the press – for example, 'a darker side to that much-vaunted transformation of Glasgow from No Mean City to Culture City' (*Sunday Times Scotland*, 13 August 1995). Others sought to prove empirically that Glasgow's murder rate was the highest in Britain; that the murders occurred in some parts but not in all parts of the city; that violence is closely linked to issues of poverty (*Scotland on Sunday*, 13 August 1995). A Labour MP declared the need to protect Glasgow's 'new' image; others claimed that the success of the image-makers had disguised the hardships still faced by many, pushing the problems of the city to the periphery – in every sense.

This episode futher illustrates the points made in the programme and the notes about the contested imagery and historical basis of competing representations of Glasgow.

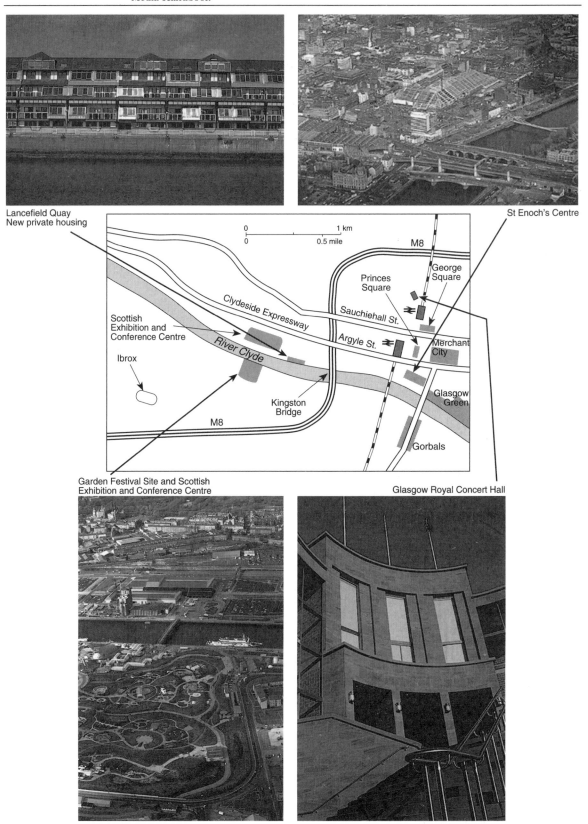

Figure 11   Glasgow city centre

Activities

Before the programme

You really need to have read Volume 4 Chapter 2 and, ideally, you will also have read Chapter 3. Try at least to have skimmed the second half of Chapter 3, section 3.3.2.

At this point it may be useful to review your response to the Activities about 'a place you know well' in Chapter 3 (Activities 1, 2, 3 and 8).

Audiocassette 3 Side A complements TV9 and ideally you will have listened to that discussion of relevant concepts.

If you have time, look again at Volume 1 Chapter 2, section 2.4 and Activity 7.

During the programme

There are two main themes to consider as you watch:

(a) *Image and identity* Note down examples of images of Glasgow. What/who is represented? What/who is *not* represented? Are there different interpretations of the images? Has this image been challenged – how and by whom?

You could use a rough matrix to help in this. For example:

Example of IMAGE	What does this REPRESENT?	How might this be INTERPRETED?	Who gains?	Who loses?	So what?

(b) *Uniqueness and interdependence* What wider (global) relationships have contributed to Glasgow's (local) character/distinctiveness?

After the programme

1   Briefly, try to develop these two themes in relation to concepts of geographical imaginations, power relations, local–global relations.

(a) Starting with your notes about images:

o   What do these images contribute to Glasgow's identity?

o   How have the images been 'constructed'?

o   Whose interests have been represented and whose suppressed?

o   How is this conflict of interests represented?

o   What do we mean by 'multiple identities'? How can a place mean more than just one thing?

o   What does all this tell us about *power relations* in Glasgow?

(b) Using your examples of local–global relationships:

o   How has Glasgow's *uniqueness* been constructed and reconstructed? What interrelationships have been involved?

o   In what ways does Glasgow's identity result from 'what Glasgow is not'? Can you relate this to the discussion of 'Othering' in Chapter 3 section 3.3 and the discussion on Audiocassette 3 Side A?

(c) Note briefly how we have used our concept of geographical imaginations to explore Glasgow's uniqueness.

2   Think about these issues in relation to another place or other places.

o   What is being represented/promoted?

o   Who gains and who loses?

Relate this to Chapter 3 Activities 1, 2, 3, 8 and other Activities in Volume 4 which ask you to consider 'a place'. (Refer also to Volume 1 Chapter 2, Activity 7.)

3 The main points to grasp from this programme are:

o that 'image and identity' are central to our geographical imagination;

o that images and identities are *socially constructed* and are not neutral or objective: how we define a place reflects and affects our attitudes towards it and our experience of it;

o that images are selective;

o that places have multiple identities;

o that images and identities are open to and reflect varied interpretations;

o that these interpretations may frequently be contested;

o that uniqueness of place is constructed out of local–global interdependencies.

Finally, Volume 4 Chapter 4 further develops ideas about contestation. Chapter 6 develops and summarizes many of the issues raised in the programme. You may find that this programme helps to illustrate some of the ideas.

References

AHMED, K. (1995) 'Glasgow reputations: powerful case for the prosecution', *Scotland on Sunday*, 13 August.

ALI, O. (1995) 'Midsummer madness makes one Mean City', *The Sunday Times Scotland*, 13 August.

ALLARDYCE, J. (1995) 'Smiling through', *The Scotsman*, 8 August.

BOLITHO, W. (1924) *Cancer of Empire*, London, Putnam.

BRYSON, B. (1989) 'Glasgow isn't Paris, but ...', *New York Times Magazine*, 9 July.

ECONOMIST, THE (1995) 'Glasgow's miles tougher', 12 August.

Acknowledgement

I would like to acknowledge the major contribution made by Gerry Mooney to the compilation of these notes and to the choice of images.

TV10 'Bajourou Mali music'

Academic Consultant: Doreen Massey

Producer: Eleanor Morris

1 Aims/links

To many people in the United Kingdom Mali may seem like one of those parts of the world which is 'off the map'. It does not figure prominently, if it figures at all, in our geographical imaginations. In fact, today, the name 'Mali' refers to a stretch of country in West Africa, stretching from the Sahara in the north to the Sahel in the south: see Figure 12. Through an important section of it winds the great bend of the River Niger. It is a land enclosed by boundaries which were laid down when it gained independent status as a country on its decolonization by France in 1960.

This is a country suffering encroaching desertification, and one of the poorest places in the world. It lies in a region which first came to European attention on the occasion of the pilgrimage to Mecca by a Malian leader in 1339. The Malian empire appeared for the first time on a European map – the Mappa Mundi of Angelino Dulcert (do you remember the *mappae mundi* of Volume 1?). At that time the term 'Mali' referred to a mighty kingdom with very different boundaries and culture from those of today. In the middle of the fourteenth century the historian Ibn Khaldun wrote of the capital of Mali as 'an extensive place, well-watered, cultivated and populated. It has brisk markets, and is now a stopping-place for trading caravans from the Maghrib, Ifriqiya and Egypt. Wares are brought here from every country' (cited in Boahen, 1986, p. 26).

In this programme we explore the relation between place and culture in present-day Mali, and we do so through some of its music. There are three parts to the argument. *First*, the question of 'Mali' as a place raises all the issues of places as meeting-places which are examined in Volume 4 Chapter 2. Mali is a place of articulation of cross-currents and contacts and influences from many areas, and a place, too, of internal variety. This is just hinted at in the programme – there are references to different influences and contacts. Some more background information is given below. *Secondly*, all this is reflected in its culture and in its musical cultures in particular. The way in which the different musical traditions of this country draw on and feed into other cultures provides an excellent laboratory for understanding tradition in terms of 'routes' and not 'roots' which is examined in Volume 4 Chapter 5. Here are examples of the phenomena of contact zones and transculturation, and more generally of hybridity, which Stuart Hall discusses in that chapter. *Thirdly*, there is the issue of the relationship between place and culture; of how attempts are made, in one way or another, to make the two conform. In discussing this issue the programme relates to Chapter 5, section 5.2 'Representing the nation', and also to the discussions in Chapter 6 of Volume 4 on the reproduction of uniqueness.

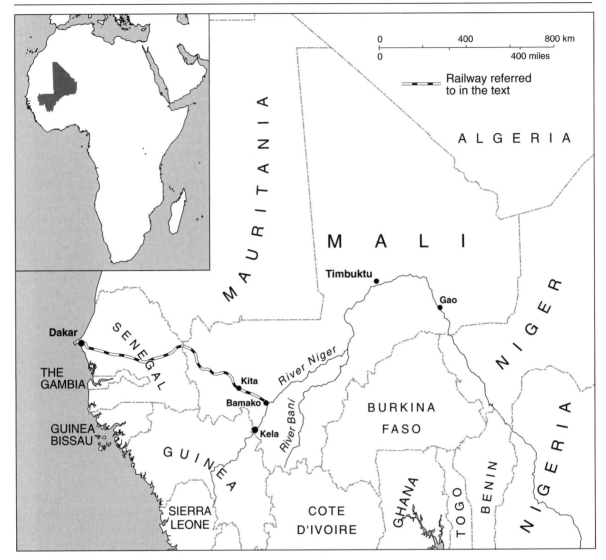

Figure 12   Mali

2   A brief history of Mali

The place which is now called Mali, and the cultures which we now call Malian are, like all other places and cultures, both internally varied and the product of contact and interaction.

As early as the third and fourth centuries AD, the communities and villages which were already thriving along the southern edge of the Sahara began to be linked into trading systems which crossed the vast expanses of desert to the north. The trans-Saharan trade, in gold, slaves, kola nuts, salt, copper, iron, dates and so on, reached its peak between the fourteenth and sixteenth centuries, and brought into contact the peoples of the Mediterranean, the Middle East and West Africa. It was, in part, with this trade that Islam spread into West Africa, bringing a new religion and new modes of social organization and literacy and culture for the ruling elites, and the growth of major cities. Jenne, Timbuktu and Gao in

Mali owe their early growth to this influence. In turn, three empires rose and fell: those of Ghana, Mali and Songhai. All of them overlapped with the country we now call Mali, but none of them coincided with its current boundaries.

As the Mali empire ceded dominance to that of Songhai, at the beginning of the fifteenth century, boats from Europe began to find their way down the west coast of Africa. The Portuguese, the Dutch, the English and the French initiated the first contacts which were to develop into full-scale colonialism by the end of the nineteenth century. It was the French who were dominant in the area now known as Mali. Mali (then called Soudan) became a French colony in 1883 and between 1896 and 1904 was part of the Federation of French West Africa, with its capital at Dakar. On independence it was briefly joined with Senegal as part of the Mali Federation. For two decades it had strong contacts with the communist bloc of Eastern Europe. Today it has the name and the boundaries you see in Figure 12, with its capital city at Bamako.

Understanding that 'potted history' is important. Above all, it indicates what insubstantial things, in some senses, 'places' are. Their characters are products of a multiplicity of influences, interacting together and reproduced over time. Their boundaries, if they have them, shift and are re-drawn in response to the power and political relations of the day. And even the name is unstable, both in itself (changing from Soudan to Mali) and in the area to which it refers (you might remember here the example of Germany as an envelope of space–time, discussed in Chapter 4).

The cultural complexity of present-day Mali reflects this history. The influences of Islam and of Europe, and of the Soviet Union and the USA, jostle with cultural forms which are more typical of sub-Saharan Africa. Within the boundaries of the nation-state a number of ethnicities co-exist (section 5.1.1). Conversely, the current boundaries cut through the geography of ethnicities: the boundary between the Côte d'Ivoire and Mali, for instance, runs through the land of the Senufo people. Although we frequently think of them as doing so, in fact, as Chapter 5 pointed out, culture and place rarely coincide.

3   The programme

The programme explores all these issues by examining music in Mali as a case study. Way back in Volume 1 Chapter 2, Richard Meegan introduced this idea of musical interchange and hybridity through his discussion of the Liverpool Sound, and Stuart Hall takes it further in Volume 4 Chapter 5. Music is of central importance to Malian culture. (Indeed it is probably underestimated in its importance to many cultures – do you remember, in Volume 4 Chapter 1, the old Greek woman in that bare hall in Sydney, Australia, her eyes closed as she danced to the music of 'her home village'?) 'Traditional' music is still powerful in Mali. The epic song 'Sunjata', deriving from the Malian empire (thirteenth century to fifteenth), is still the most important song in every traditional musician's repertoire. Music is part of the social structure: a separate caste – the *jalis* – are the country's musicians. And music is still central to all ceremonies, and the women singers of the traditional songs are major national stars.

Sunset over Bamako, the capital of Mali. The River Niger flows through the heart of Africa, but is crossed by a Russian-built bridge and the skyscraper is a Middle-Eastern bank – an illustration of the theme of hybridity

But this 'traditional' music is itself complex; it itself contains a multiplicity of influences. Reviews speak of its 'Arabic edge'. The 'local' instrument, the *ngoni* (an oblong lute), can be found throughout the West African savannah, and may have originated in Egypt. There are colonial influences from France and – very importantly – links with Cuban music. Indeed, in a classic example of tradition through routes, it seems that some elements of Cuban music were originally taken *to* that country by Manding people when they were transported there in the slave trade (Volume 1 Chapter 2 and Volume 4 Chapters 1 and 5). The recent importation is thus of music which was once exported but which returns having been changed *en route*. More recently, influences from the United States of America have been significant.

The music of Mali is locked into changing sets of links with other places. And those links have not just been inward. The cultural influence of Mali music has also spread outwards. The slaves took not only music to the 'New World' but also instruments. The *ngoni* was recreated on the other side of the Atlantic as the banjo. The migration of people from Mali to France led to a thriving culture in Paris. And today's globalization of the music industry sees not only the influx of Western music to Mali but the growing knowledge and recognition of Malian music around the world. It is an important contributor to 'world music'.

The programme follows a trio of Mali musicians who are important players in this globalization. The music that they play, and the name of the trio itself, is *Bajourou*. Bajourou is an explicit attempt to continue this building of tradition through contact, through routes; to reproduce uniqueness by binding in new elements from 'outside'. These new elements are used, subverted and adapted in a process of transculturation. Bajourou music links inherited forms to new 'modern' western imports, to produce something new but something still definitely of Mali.

In the programme we follow the group in order to explore the themes outlined above. Each member of the trio has something different to tell us about the complex and evolving links between culture and place.

Lafia Diabate, the singer, has strong roots in traditional Maninka music and dance. He is part of an extended family of *jalis*, and takes us back to his village (Kela) in southern Mali, near the border with Guinea. This village lies in what was the heart of the old Malian empire, whose boundaries stretched across the borders of modern nation-states. Here the music is integral to the life of the village, and the traditional *ngoni* is an important instrument.

Lafia's village, in an area that was within the old kingdom of Mali. Through the arch can be seen the local mosque, showing that it is also part of the Islamic world

Jalimadi Tounkara is also a *jali* whose early musical experience was traditional. His village is near the town of Kita, an old French colonial town. Jalimadi takes us there on a railway built by the French to link Dakar on the coast to Bamako on the River Niger (remember the notion of 'contact zone' in Chapter 5?). (The importance of this railway is indicated by the existence of the Rail Band.) The route of Jalimadi's life, however, took him on from there to incorporate other western influences. He tells us he has been strongly influenced by US music.

Bouba Sacko, like Jalimadi, is a guitarist. He too has roots in traditional music, having accompanied many of Mali's women singers. He continues to play at celebrations such as weddings. Bouba reflects on the importance of music in Malian society – its importance in daily life and in bringing the different ethnic groups together. He speaks of how music has been a factor 'making the nation'. His personal history is different again and enables us to explore a further aspect of the relation between culture and place.

While the European Cup Winners' Cup Final was being watched on a television in his village, Bouba was playing traditional African music to the programme-makers

Bouba Sacko's father was a founder of Mali's *National Ensemble*. This state-subsidized ensemble of traditional musicians was part of an attempt to build a sense of national culture in the years after independence (remember Stuart Hall's discussion of Jamaica in Volume 4 Chapter 5). Although the boundaries of the colony had little to do with old ethnicities and loyalties, colonialism itself – and the fight for independence – gave birth to a new nationalism. But a sense of place had to be created, a national community had to be imagined (see Chapter 5, section 5.2). In Mali, as it has been elsewhere, music was a significant element in that attempt to build a geographical imagination of the nation. Indeed, that is, in part, what Bajourou continues to be about today – the building of a new hybrid cultural identity which is still uniquely of this place.

Yet, at the same time, musical culture is constantly a mixture, and a culture with no frontiers. Bouba speaks both of the wide geographical roots/routes of 'traditional' music and of the travels abroad which the group itself now undertakes. His reflections in particular enable us to ponder the ever-shifting relations between 'culture' and 'place'.

Activities

Before the programme

You should have read Volume 4 Chapter 5. If you have time, check up on what Stuart Hall says about the reformulation of the notion of culture (section 5.3.1).

During the programme

As you watch, try to pick out instances of hybridity and of transculturation. And keep your eyes open for instances of the non-coincidence of culture and place.

After the programme

1   Try to relate Mali music to Stuart Hall's re-conceptualization of the concept of culture.

2   Then try to relate this to the reformulation of the concept of place in Volume 4 Chapter 2. This is not easy, and the aim is really to bring home to yourself the complexity of the links between place and culture. Chapter 6 of Volume 4 should help you to develop these thoughts further.

Reference

BOAHEN, A. (1986) *Topics in West African History*, Harlow, Longman.

TV11 'Changing Berlin, changing Europe?'

Academic consultant: Allan Cochrane

Producer: Jack Leathem

1 Aims/links

The main aim of this programme is to explore the complex relationships which link 'local' experiences to 'global' changes. To do this we use a historical case study of Berlin in the twentieth century, particularly since 1945, charting some of the different roles which Berlin has played within Germany and Europe. The intention is to highlight the ways in which global political and economic changes have helped to set the context within which Berlin has developed its identities, and to show some of the ways in which Berlin's residents have sought to define and redefine the place in which they live. 'Local' initiative has helped to influence apparently 'global' processes, while 'global' changes have in turn set the context for 'local' initiative.

Just as images and representations of Berlin have changed over the twentieth century, so the nature of the 'Europe' of which it is a part has also changed. A subsidiary aim of the programme is to consider some implications of this. Berlin began the century as the capital of an imperial nation within a Europe of independent states; for a brief moment in the 1940s it became capital of Nazi Europe; after 1945 it was a symbol of a divided Europe in the context of the Cold War; and in 1989 it took on a new symbolism with the collapse of communism and the apparent integration of Eastern Europe into what used to be called western capitalism. The question remains whether Berlin is now an outpost of Western Europe (and the European Union) at the gateway to the East, or at the centre of a new Europe which stretches from the Atlantic to the Urals (see Figure 13).

The programme is directly linked to arguments in Volume 5 of the course, and specifically to discussions in Chapter 6, 'Global worlds and worlds of difference', because of the ways in which it focuses on the re-ordering of Berlin's own 'local' political space, and the re-ordering of the 'global' political space in which it is located. It also highlights the relationship of one place (Berlin) to changes taking place within the European macro-, or global, region. It complements the discussions about these issues which take place in Chapter 3, where Chris Brook explores the 'drive to global regions' and that of Europe in particular. As you watch the programme, you should therefore pay particular attention to these issues, with the case of Berlin being used to explore the active processes through which politics is shaped and reshaped locally in a wider regional and global context.

It is, however, also worth pointing out that, not surprisingly at this stage of the course, the issues raised in the programme are highly relevant to discussions earlier in the course, not only in Volume 1, where the connections between 'local' and 'global' aspects of representation are interrogated, but also in Volume 2, where notions of 'global' cities and transnational linkages are explored, and in Volume 4, where issues of

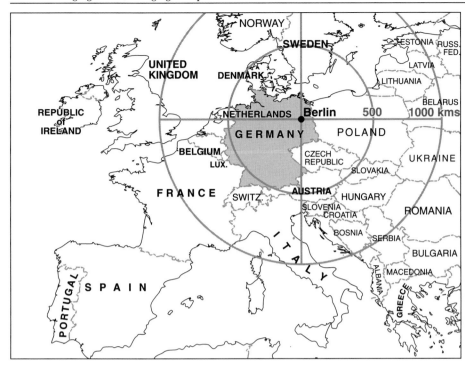

Figure 13 *Berlin: at the heart of Europe?*

place and culture are the central focus of attention. So it is important not to put the programme just in a box labelled Volume 5, but to use it to explore further some of the key themes of the course in a different context.

2   The programme

As already outlined, Berlin has been at the centre of a dramatic series of changes through the twentieth century and the programme focuses on them, not just as a historical narrative, but rather to illustrate the power of some of the themes developed in the course. Berlin has changed and continues to change through a constant process of interpretation and reinterpretation, as an expression of different (often competing) geographical imaginations.

2.1   From Prussian capital to outpost of 'the West'

The symbolic importance of a changing Berlin within a changing Europe lies at the heart of the programme. Berlin began the twentieth century a little uncertain of its great city status. It had only recently become the capital of a unified (and imperial) Germany, having previously been no more than the capital of the kingdom of Prussia. The Prussian aristocracy had never entirely trusted big city life and few of them had permanent homes in Berlin. According to Nicholas Sombart, a historian whom we interview in the programme, despite the city's formal importance and the siting of the Reichstag within it, Berlin remained relatively provincial – a stopping-off place through which cultured Russians passed on their way from Moscow to Paris. In the inter-war Weimar period of the 1920s, Berlin became for a brief moment a rival to Paris, a centre of Bohemianism and even decadence. It became a European city, as well as capital of Germany, and an industrial centre with a strong left-wing tradition.

After 1933 all this began to change. Within Germany the Nazis sought to put their stamp on Berlin, to show that they had defeated the cosmopolitanism and radicalism with which the city was popularly associated. The Jewish population was, of course, a prime target of attention, but as a traditional base of the Social Democratic Party, the transformation of Berlin into the capital first of a centralized Nazi Germany and then of a Nazi Europe also required extensive changes to the fabric of the city. The architecture of power expressed in the Nazis' buildings (such as the Olympiastadion built for the 1936 Olympics), and their use of boulevards like Unter den Linden for massive parades, helped to stamp the image of their rule on the physical geography of the city. And Hitler had still more grandiose plans for the reconstruction of Berlin under the new name of Germania, in order to confirm his rule and the power of his will in reshaping Germany. The scars of Hitler's plans are still to be seen in extensive dereliction in the centre of the city (near the Reichstag), in part preserved through the later siting of the Berlin Wall to cut across it (see Figure 14).

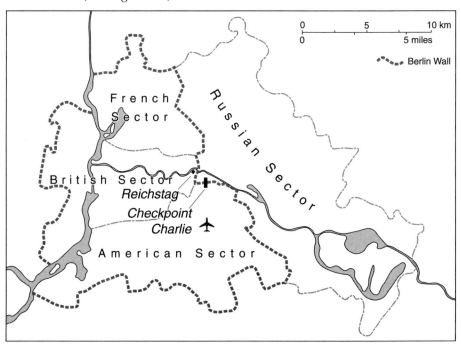

Figure 14 Berlin: the former sectors and siting of the Wall

At the end of the Second World War, of course, Berlin continued to play a key role in global imagery. It was the raising of the Red Flag on the roof of the Reichstag that symbolized the complete and final victory of the Allies over Germany (even if it took a bit longer before Soviet troops actually gained control of the building). And it also symbolized the beginning of a new bi-polar world of global politics, because it highlighted the role of the Soviet Union in determining what was possible in Europe. Throughout the Cold War period the politics of global conflict often found its most powerful expressions in images drawn from Berlin.

After 1945 the city became an island, at first within the Soviet-occupied zone of Germany, but soon within the 'people's democracy' of the German Democratic Republic (of East Germany), so named in contrast to the Federal Republic of Germany (or West Germany). At first the city was divided into four zones, each run by the military forces of the victorious allies (the UK, France, the USA and the Soviet Union), but later East Berlin was absorbed into the German Democratic Republic (as capital) while West Berlin had its own governing system (with Senate and Burgermeister) and a close relationship to the Federal Republic. The fiction that Berlin was under military rule, however, survived in some form, with officers of the different forces continuing to meet, and garrisons being maintained until the early 1990s.

Soviet soldier hoisting the Soviet flag on the burnt-out building of the Reichstag, 30 April 1945, symbolizing the victory of the Russian army

2.2 A symbol of capitalism and showcase of communism

Throughout the post-war period Berlin was a flash-point in the political conflicts of the Cold War. At first the Soviet Union attempted to isolate West Berlin and make it unmanageable. A blockade was imposed on road and rail transport, but an airlift was organized by the western powers to ensure that supplies continued to get through. Later, in 1961, the Cold War seemed to be given physical form with the building of the Berlin Wall by the East German government. In the early 1960s President Kennedy went to the city to proclaim that he, too, was a 'Berliner' (only later discovering that this was a popular form of doughnut), committing the USA to defend West Berlin against perceived threats of Russian expansionism. In 1989 it was the fall of the Berlin Wall – transmitted around the world on television and on the front page of every newspaper – and the subsequent reunification of city and state which finally confirmed the collapse of the Soviet bloc. The put-put of East German two-stroke cars (the Trabants or Trabis), as they queued to cross into West Berlin, sounded the death-knell for the bipolar world of superpower conflict and accommodation between the USA and the Soviet Union.

Berlin's global significance had far-reaching local consequences, some of which are explored in the programme. West Berlin became an island of capitalism in the sea of East German communism. It was a thriving city heavily subsidized by the West, alive twenty-four hours a day, an outpost of glitter and consumerism in the front-line of the Cold War. Paradoxically, however, despite this front-line status, because it was not formally part of the Federal Republic, local residents did not have to undertake military service, so the city also became a place of refuge for young people seeking to avoid conscription and by the 1960s it had a thriving alternative political culture. West Berlin also became home for a large Turkish community, whose members were able to find work in a city made prosperous by state policy and global politics, but a city artificially cut off from its own hinterland for the same reasons.

By contrast, East Berlin – as capital city of the German Democratic Republic – was increasingly presented as a showcase of the success of communism, with major construction schemes used to give physical expression to the system in the form of grand boulevards like the Karl Marxallee and the building of the Alexanderturm – transmitting radio and television programmes and reaching into the sky as symbol of technological advance in the 1960s. Because of its position as capital, East Berlin was a place in which there was frequent interaction between East and West. Although the biggest dissident campaigns in East Germany started in other big cities (such as Leipzig and Dresden), they soon also found an expression in Berlin, even though it was the home of government and state power.

2.3   Reunification: effects and prospects

The programme explores the ways in which global changes have influenced and shaped the life-experiences of people living in Berlin by looking at them through the eyes of two families. One of these – the Domroses – lives in East Berlin and the other – the Gartlegrubers – in West Berlin. It will be clear from the programme that even within similar family groups the changes have had differential effects, although there have been new problems for members of both families alongside new opportunities for some. For Ulli Domrose the abolition of the Wall has created literally global opportunities as his collection of East German photography was in high demand outside the country – resulting in exhibitions in the US and elsewhere in Europe. For Christienne Domrose, opportunities have been more restricted, as subsidies to cultural activities in Berlin have been reduced and her skills in scenery painting are no longer in demand. Like Christienne Domrose, Michael Gartlegruber had worked in the cultural industries. Like her, too, the withdrawal of subsidies has severely reduced his employment prospects. Sabine Gartlegruber has been affected rather differently by economic difficulties arising from unification, as it becomes more difficult to maintain an adequate income from her snack and tobacco kiosk.

The fall of the Berlin Wall, 1989

The re-emergence of Berlin as an 'ordinary' place, able to make its own history, has generated significant problems of adjustment, some of which are highlighted in these individual experiences. The children of both families seem more ready to take the new situation for granted. For one of them the fall of the Wall clearly took second place to the celebration of her birthday on the same day. An exploration of the tensions associated with change and the search for new forms of economic, political and cultural arrangements run through the programme. For the Turkish community, the changed world brings new threats, from increased economic uncertainty that is also frequently expressed through the impact of racism and racist movements. Turkish people face increased danger of racist attack and some – like one of the footballers we interview in the programme – even argue that it might have been better if the Wall had never come down. The city itself faces major restructuring: the centre is being redeveloped and the 'green' image of West Berlin (preserved in the aspic of the post-war boundaries) is being eroded by massively increased traffic flows. Meanwhile, economic uncertainty is undermining the old securities of East and West Berliners.

The search is on for a new role in the future, one which links local aspirations to the changed world within which they may be realized. The Federal government has already agreed to move the capital back to Berlin, despite the misgivings of some of its civil servants. But this is only a first step in redefining the status of Berlin within the new world. For some local residents it seems a threat as much as an opportunity, because it seems to imply a move away from federalism to a more centralized and unified nation. They fear that the relative openness and social tolerance of the past (at least in what was West Berlin) may be replaced by increased discipline and policing to protect the state institutions which are to be housed in Berlin.

2.4   An uncertain future

There is a high degree of uncertainty about the future. It is widely recognized that the future of Berlin will depend on its position within the global system. But local politicians and residents still need to clarify what the options are, as they attempt to develop strategies for place marketing within a highly competitive market-place. Many hope that Berlin will become the capital of a new Europe which is capable of incorporating the states previously trapped within the Soviet bloc. It is often argued that the city is particularly well placed for such a development – close to the Polish border, with some linkages surviving from the old Soviet system. It is in a special situation because it encapsulates within its boundaries the experiences of capitalism and communism. Berlin, it is argued, can be seen as a bridge between Eastern and Western Europe, between the emerging market economies of Central Europe and Russia and the established capitalist leaders of the European Union.

More pessimistically, however, some fear that in moving away from its past position on the world stage, Berlin may simply become marginalized on the edge of a powerful Western European economic bloc. Instead of acting as a bridge, it may end up with the role of policing the West's borders with the less secure economies of Eastern and Central Europe. Instead of being in the front-line of the Cold War, Berlin may soon be in the front-line of immigration control, stopping the feared influx from Poland and beyond, into the heartlands of the West. The moving of the Bundestag from Bonn to Berlin may be a necessary element in any strategy to avoid this scenario, but it will not be enough. At the turn of the century, many of Germany's rulers avoided setting up permanent residence in the city. Now the fear must be that Berlin will formally become capital once more, but may not take on all the functions expected of a capital city. Bonn is not Germany's financial, industrial nor cultural capital and is the most resolutely suburban of Europe's capital cities. It is therefore unlikely that Berlin will gain these other functions simply because it takes on Bonn's political role.

Activities

Before the programme

It is unlikely that you will have had the chance to read Chapter 6 of Volume 5 before viewing this programme, and you should not worry if you have not done so. The Introduction to Volume 5 will be helpful, however, and a reading of Chapter 3 will help you to focus on some of the wider changes taking place within Europe. This programme picks up on many of the issues developed earlier in the course and sets out to build on them in the particular context of Berlin's changing role within a changing global and European context. It should, therefore, help you to review many of the key debates of the course, particularly as they relate to the networks of connections which stretch across space, linking local and global processes of change.

During the programme

There are three main issues on which you should focus as you watch the programme:

(a)   the ways in which places such as Berlin (and the experiences of people living in them) are shaped by their position within changing global political arrangements;

(b)   the ways in which apparently local initiatives may themselves help to shape and influence global change;

(c) arising from the first two, the interconnectedness and interrelationship between global and local processes (for example, in the ways in which people living in Berlin define themselves).

After the programme

Chapter 6 of Volume 5 explicitly returns to many of the issues raised in this programme and Activity 3 specifically relates to Berlin. When you reach that point in the course it will be helpful to think back to this programme, so it might be worth taking a few notes, first to remind yourself of the changing roles which Berlin has played in Europe through the twentieth century and, secondly, to consider their implications for the city and where possible for those living in it. My own list of the changing roles is roughly as follows:

o capital of imperial Germany

o cultural capital in the 1920s

o capital of Nazi Germany and Nazi Europe

o Berlin as global symbol of the Cold War

o West Berlin as capitalist island in a communist sea

o East Berlin as capital of communist state

o fall of the Berlin Wall as symbol

o looking for a new role in a changing Europe.

The experience of Berlin highlights in a particularly sharp form the need to bring together global and local concerns in the analysis of social and political change. It is the relationship between them that helps to shape the context within which we all live our lives. It might finally be worth considering just how much scope Berlin's politicians and residents have for redefining the city through a process of place marketing in ways that will allow it (and them) to benefit from the reshaping of Europe which is taking place in the wake of the collapse of the Soviet bloc.

TV12 'The world of the dragon'

Academic consultant: John Allen

Producer: Eleanor Morris

1 Aims/links

The main aim of this programme is to draw attention to a part of the world whose future holds a series of consequences for how those of us in the West think about global and local change. Whilst it is obviously difficult to highlight future trends and consequences with any degree of accuracy, it is possible that what is happening in the East today, in particular in China and in East Asia, will disrupt any simple notions of East and West that we may hold and, more significantly, displace western-centred views of globalization.

This disruption takes as its focus the transformations that are being wrought in China as it attempts to shift from a poor and backward nation to the world's next economic superpower in little over a decade. Rapid change, initiated by Premier Deng Xiaoping's 'open door' reforms in 1979, has come about as much by internal political and economic reforms as it has by investment decisions taken outside China. There has been a massive surge of interest by western multinationals in setting up operations in what has the potential to be the world's biggest consumer market. The vast majority of investment has come not from the West, however, but from the 'Overseas Chinese' – ethnic Chinese living outside China, in particular in Hong Kong, Taiwan, South East Asia and North America.

Investments from these groups of Overseas Chinese dominate the flow of foreign capital into China and 'collectively' they represent a network of connections unlike those in the West. It is this network of connections, a kind of transnational Chinese economy, that occupies a central role in the programme and offers an insight into how global relationships can take different forms from those in the West.

The programme is linked directly with the kinds of transnational relationships discussed and illustrated in Volume 5, especially those which cut across conventional political and economic boundaries. It offers another illustration of the fact that there are many different ways of stretching relationships across the globe. When you come to read the final chapter in Volume 5, you will find many of these illustrations summarized in the context of changing local and global relations. Having said that, the programme material will not be unfamiliar to you. The topic of the Overseas Chinese was discussed briefly in Chapter 3 of Volume 1, which bears a similar title to Volume 5, namely 'Global worlds'. There the Overseas Chinese network was considered as one which did cut across Western social space and the chapter raised the prospect of thinking about globalization in a non-western way. Stretching our global imaginations in this way is precisely what this programme is all about. As such, it ends the series of television programmes in the same way that TV1 began it: namely, by exploring and developing one of the key concepts of the course – our geographical imaginations.

2   The programme

Whereas TV1 involved a journey through eastern Mexico that unravelled the global and historical connections which had shaped that particular place, the emphasis in this programme is upon the kinds of connections which are shaping China's future. Shanghai, the largest city in China with a population of just under 13 million, carries much of the initial storyline and provides an illustration of how China is being 'opened up' today. At the head of the Yangtse River basin, Shanghai – the 'dragon head' – is once again 'roaring' economically. After a decade or more of being held back economically by the Chinese Communist Party, Shanghai is attempting to regain its status as the premier industrial and export powerhouse of China. Overtaken by the likes of Guangdong province and the Shenzen economic zone in the south (situated close to Hong Kong), Shanghai is now engaged in a race to catch up. A much quoted aim of the city is, by the year 2010, to have overtaken Hong Kong as a financial centre and trading giant – ironically the very city to which many Shanghaiese entrepreneurs fled in 1949 in their rush to escape the onset of Communist rule.

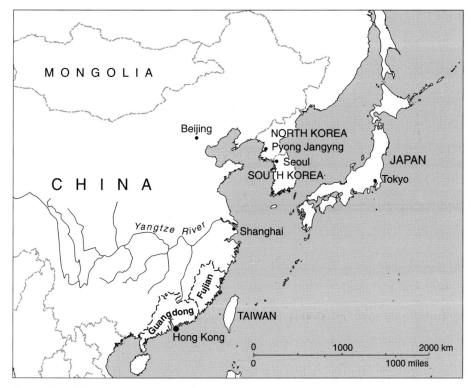

Figure 15   *China – on the Pacific Rim*

It is this migration of Chinese overseas, a pattern which has repeated itself historically many times, which takes up and moves on the storyline, linking the Chinese diaspora to the potential economic giant that China is today. As the programme suggests, this transnational network of connections represents the lifeblood of the Chinese business world – a world global in its reach and locked into places like Shanghai.

2.1 Shanghai: the 'dragon head'

One of the most striking images of Shanghai (and indeed a mark of uneven and interdependent development), however, is not its Chinese characteristics but its western symbols. The Bund, the classic river frontage of what was once the International Concession, stands as a testament to the fact that the rest of the world has long been in Shanghai. Always the Chinese city most open to the outside world, a short walk along the Bund reveals some classic 1920s buildings: the old Hong Kong and Shanghai Bank, the Peace Hotel (with its art deco designs and nightly jazz band), the Shanghai Club (of which to be a member in the 1920s you had to be white, male and preferably British), and the old Astor Hotel.

The Bund waterfront in 1927, showing the Hong Kong and Shanghai Bank (with the large dome) and various newspaper and shipping offices, mostly under the control of foreigners from the West

Today, the ballroom of the Astor Hotel dances to a different rhythm – that of global finance: as the home of Shanghai's stock exchange its key is taken from the Jingan financial index rather than from a western dance orchestra. This transformation is likely to be shortlived nevertheless, as the bulk of Shanghai's financial activities is to move to the city's special economic zone, Pudong New Development Area (see Figure 16). On Pudong rest the hopes of development of Shanghai and the Yangtze River valley basin into the twenty-first century. Comprising some five separate zones, areas like the Jingqiao Export Processing Zone play host to a range of western firms, including electronics giants such as Philips, Siemens and Sharp.

Western firms like these are not in Pudong, or elsewhere in China for that matter, simply to take advantage of cheaper labour costs, however. China is potentially one of the largest consumer markets in the world and many

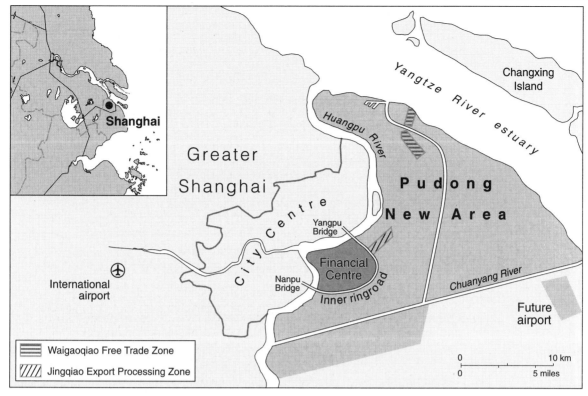

Figure 16 *Pudong New Area on the other side of the Huangpu River from Shanghai*

western firms regard it as imperative that they have a presence (even if it means trading at a loss initially). Volkswagen and their Santana model have a head-start in what promises to be an exploding car market. Economists note that if China is able to produce 1.5 million cars a year by 2010, this would still leave private car ownership at only around 2.2 per cent of the 270 million Chinese families. Likewise in telecommunications the market is potentially vast: if China reaches its target of installing 11 million lines a year up until 2000, it will have added the equivalent of the UK's total phone network every three years. It is not surprising, then, that the global telecommunications firms, such as AT&T, Motorola, Ericsson, Alcatel and Northern Telecom, are all investing heavily in joint ventures with Chinese partners.

It would be wrong, however, to think that this was largely a western affair. As the programme points out (and noted above), the flow of investment coming into China is dominated by Overseas Chinese entrepreneurs, not western firms. In Pudong, for instance, nearly two-thirds of investment can be traced to firms based in Hong Kong. Indeed, Hong Kong acts as a springboard for the Overseas Chinese to do business in mainland China, especially those from Taiwan. In the programme, for example, you will meet the Hsu Bin family who left Shanghai in 1949 to settle in Taiwan and who are now among the prominent investors in Pudong, ranging from industrial projects to commercial housing and offices. The ties of the family to Shanghai are strong, as are those of many businesses from Taiwan, and it is these connections and others like them which account for much of the contemporary dynamism of the city. There may have been a 'gold rush' of foreign investors, but on closer inspection the majority of the 'foreigners' are ethnic Chinese living outside China.

2.2 The Overseas Chinese network

The Overseas Chinese number some 55 million and comprise a variety of ethnicities and languages. The majority are to be found in Hong Kong and Taiwan, although elsewhere in East Asia they have a significant presence. The vast majority of Singaporeans are Mandarin-speaking Chinese, for example, and countries like Malaysia, Thailand, Indonesia and the Philippines have economically powerful Chinese minorities. Collectively their investment flows in the East Asia region are larger than that of Japan, and the network has been likened to a kind of borderless economy connecting the major Asian cities. As the programme shows, the network stretches beyond Asia, taking in places like Vancouver in North America, but it is not the scope of investments which distinguishes it from western networks: it is the way it operates and its very character.

2.2.1 The family connection

Overseas Chinese businesses, even when they take the form of listed companies, are dominated by family connections. Often highly decentralized, yet autocratically run, the ties of kinship – loosely translated to include clan or village of origin – shape the organizations of the Overseas Chinese. Li Kai-Shing's empire across East Asia and beyond is closer to western managerial forms, but family control is still paramount – as is the case with the Kuok family's holdings (see Figure 17). Most Overseas Chinese businesses are, however, small in size and dominated by family networks across space.

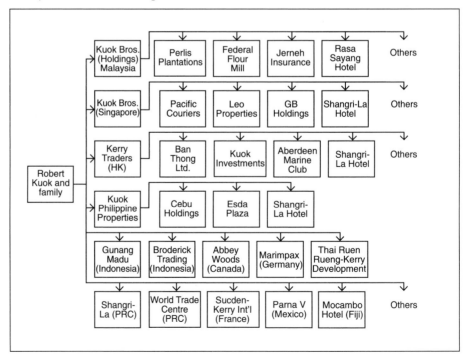

Figure 17   *The Kuok family's holdings*

2.2.2 Guanxi

Guanxi refers to the informal nature of the connections within and between families in the network which enables business to be conducted 'at a distance'. Trust and obligation play a central role in the networks, both sustaining relationships across different parts of the globe and also 'opening up' investments in different places. Overseas Chinese money pouring back into China tends to flow back to the villages and provinces with which the family has a connection: much of the money from Hong Kong, for example, has been invested in Guangdong, and the majority of funds from Taiwan has gone to Fuijian. In each instance, the family connections direct the flow of investment (and people, too).

2.2.3 The next generation

The networks are far from static, however, and a second generation of Overseas Chinese is now interlaced with the first. Business is no longer limited to those who share a common ancestry, yet the ties of family still predominate. *Guanxi* may operate through state-of-the-art telecommunications, but it is still trust and not fibre-optic cables which actually overcomes distance. Technology may annihilate space, but the ability to conduct relationships swiftly and smoothly across national borders relies upon informal 'blood' connections.

In the programme, we travel to Vancouver to look at the way in which the Hui family transcends space, as it were, through family connections and note that the Chinese diaspora is neither a new phenomenon, nor unique in its global scale. What distinguishes it today is the forms of family and business which the Overseas Chinese operate: they represent a network of connections to which the West is only a bystander. Even much of the money that flows through the network is generated by the network itself, rather than raised by public listings or from western banks – for fear of ceding control to outside interests.

2.3 Globalization – eastern-style?

At the end of the programme, the question is raised as to the nature of connections which make up the transnational Chinese economy. As most of our models of globalization are based on western-centred models, it raises the question of whether we would recognize other forms – forms which have taken shape in non-western cultures. If we wish to understand what is happening in dynamic parts of the world like China and East Asia today, is it a problem that we are imagining it from 'here' rather than from 'there'? Having reached the end of this course, it should come as no surprise to you that there is more than one global imagination.

Activities

Before the programme

Re-read section 3.3.3 of Volume 1, 'Other worlds', and then think carefully about the way in which Islamic imaginations may attempt to understand global relationships. Brian Beeley's account of Islam in Chapter 4 of Volume 5 will help you here. After that, consider carefully how the example of the Overseas Chinese network may 'stretch' relationships across the globe in ways different from those of western businesses.

During the programme

There are two particular aspects that you should look out for as you watch the programme.

The *first* is the different ways in which 'external' connections have shaped the fortunes and character of Shanghai over the years. Of course, not all the significant factors will be external, but the different connections will give you an insight into how Shanghai has been shaped and re-shaped over time.

The *second* aspect to look out for concerns the make-up of the Overseas Chinese network – *what flows through it and how does it hold together?* And, related to this, how has it changed?

After the programme

Finally, think about the significance of the point raised in section 2.3 above. Are we looking at a form of eastern-style globalization? If you think so, reflect upon the kind of knowledge that makes up a western geographical imagination.

Acknowledgements

Grateful acknowledgement is made to the following sources for permission to use the following photographs in this Handbook:

p.12: Bertelsmann Aktiengesellschaft, CNN International/Turner Broadcasting System Ltd, News International, Time Warner; *p. 25:* Popperfoto; *p. 37:* Barbara Smith; *pp. 48, 49:* Steve Pile; *p. 55:* riveter based on the cover of the exhibition catalogue for 'Clydebuilt: The River, its Ships and its People', organized by the Clyde Maritime Trust Ltd.; *p. 56:* *Glasgow Herald*/Caledonian Newspapers Limited; *p. 57: (logos) (top)* Mr Happy adaptation: Mr Men and Little Miss^{TM} and © 1995 Mrs Roger Hargreaves, *(all)* Courtesy: City of Glasgow; *p. 57: (bottom) (left)* City of Glasgow, *(middle)* Courtesy: The Citizen, *(right)* source unknown; *p. 59:* Courtesy of *Corporate Location* Magazine; *p. 60: (both)* © Alan Wylie Photographer; *p. 62: (top left and right, and bottom left)* Glasgow Development Agency, *(bottom right)* © Alan Crumlish; *p. 75:* Popperfoto; *p. 77:* © Justin Leighton/Network; *p. 82:* © Hulton Deutsch; *p. 83:* 'Shanghai', *Business China Supplement,* Autumn 1993, Copyright © by the The Economist Intelligence Unit (Asia) Ltd.; *p. 85:* © David Ch'ng/The Committee for Economic Development of Australia (CEDA).

Every effort has been made to trace all copyright holders. If further information can be supplied to amend any acknowledgements, the publishers will be pleased to do so at the first opportunity.